GASTRONOMES, 2

GASTRONOMES
Series editor Marco Pace Brin
«Gastronomes» is a series exploring the history of cuisine. Each book reveals the history and culture of an important topic related to food and its preparation.

First edition April 2023
COPYRIGHT © 2023 GASTRONOMES
Twitter.com/gastronomes_US
All rights reserved. No part of this publication may be reproduced, stored in a retrieval system, or transmitted, in any form or by any means, electronic, mechanical, photocopying, recording or otherwise, except as permitted by the US Copyright, without the prior permission of the publisher.

Limitation of liability/Disclaimer of warranty: while the publisher and author have used their best efforts in preparing this book, they make no representations or warranties with respect to the accuracy or completeness of the contents of this book and specifically disclaim any implied warranties of merchantability or fitness for a particular purpose. It is sold on the understanding that the publisher is not engaged in rendering professional services and neither the publisher nor the author shall be liable for damages arising herefrom. If professional advice or other expert assistance is required, the services of a competent professional should be sought.

Cover image by Nikodem Nijaki — Travail personnel, CC BY-SA 3.0, https://commons.wikimedia.org/w/index.php?curid=16837378
COVER DESIGN: THE GASTRONOMES

FOIE GRAS: 138 RECIPES
EDITED BY MARCO PACE BRIN

The Gastronomes

Foie gras: about

This cookbook is (relatively) big, given it contains 138 recipes, distributed within more than 200 pages, dedicated to just one ingredient: Foie gras.

But what actually surprised me while compiling the book was to see how few recipes were dedicated to this noble ingredient. Let me explain.

A few words about this series

There is a difference between this cookbook and (well, nearly) all others seen before: instead of concentrating its duty in the preparation of each recipe, this one concentrates on putting together the culinary history of foie gras.

It is the same for each book in the series: the enormous quantity of recipes presented here (if thought in relationship with a single ingredient) is not assisted (as usual in our times) by a rich set of illustrations and instructions that allows anyone to execute the recipe. It is mainly because the recipes come from reliable and certified sources: an impressive number of cookbooks chosen from the most authoritative published in the English language over the last three hundred years. Hence, these recipes pertain to the history of cuisine.

And this is why I wrote that I had been surprised: basically, the recipes collected in this book are reasonably all the ones that in the history of cuisine have been prepared with this ingredient. In the end, very few.

Some recipes collected in this book are complicated. The complicacy derives not only from the difficulties in preparation, but from the way text is arranged: as one may know, cook writers of the past weren't so punctilious about writing precise instructions on how to prepare a meal. They reasonably referred to a professional public: a public of cooks: in most of the cases the author skirts the issue when it is time to give the exact quantities and a step by step procedure about how to reproduce the recipe. It is the limit of the book. Since very recent times only (let's say, since 1950s?) cookbook writers matured a sensibility about explaining in plain English to the general public how to prepare a meal.

To keep things short, you'll frequently have to exercise a bit your fantasy. If this sacrifice as a reader sounds reasonable to you, you will get compensated: not only you will find in this book the whole set of foundational recipes about using foie gras; you'll enjoy the eccentricities, habits, elegance of grand cooks.

All notes are from the editor.

Now about the foie gras

Foie gras is a culinary specialty made from fresh liver from the breeding and fattening by force-feeding of geese and ducks, a popular and well-known festive delicacy in French cuisine. It is eaten raw, semi-cooked or cooked, and can be offered as fresh or canned products, eaten alone or as an accompaniment to other dishes such as meat. According to French law, "foie gras is part of the cultural and gastronomic heritage protected in France. By foie gras we mean the liver of a duck or a goose specially fattened by force-feeding".

If the force-feeding technique dates from when the ancient Egyptians began to force-feed birds to fatten them up, the consumption of foie gras itself was first reported in ancient Rome.

Today, France is by far the largest producer and consumer of foie gras, followed by the rest of Europe, the United States and China.

Due to controversies over animal force-feeding, several countries or jurisdictions have enacted laws against the production or marketing of products obtained by force-feeding under pressure from animal welfare groups. An alternative is to recognize and promote natural force-feeding.

Its history

Depicted in the 4,500-year-old tomb frescoes at Saqqara, the practice of force-feeding geese dates back at least to ancient Egypt. The Egyptians force-fed several species of web-footed birds, including geese, using roasted and moistened grain pellets. The practice continued in ancient Greece and under the Roman Empire. Athenaeus and several authors of the Greek theater report in their writings the Greek practice of fattening palmipeds with wheat crushed in water. Pliny the Elder evokes the force- feeding of geese among the Romans using balls of dried and crushed figs, soaked for 20 days to soften them. In the 4th century, the *De re coquinaria* of Apicius gives its first recipe. The liver produced was called in Latin *Jecur ficatum*, which is literally translated as "liver with figs". The ancients kept only the term *ficatum* or *fig* for its denomination, which gave the form *figido* in the 8th century, then *fedie, feie* in the 12th and finally *foie* ("liver"). This root is found in Romance languages, such as French, Italian, Portuguese, Spanish and Romanian. From the 5th century to the 16th century, there are few written or iconographic traces of foie gras and its production methods. The tradition of foie gras continued after the fall of the Roman Empire in central Europe, in Jewish communities. The Jews frequently used goose fat for cooking, as butter with meat and lard was forbidden to them. Additionally, olive and sesame oils were difficult to obtain in Central and Western Europe. The Jews spread the breeding of geese, from Alsace to the Urals, and learned to master force-feeding.

In France, the industrialization of production took place from the 1980s in relation to mass distribution, industrialists started to produce foie gras and duck confit on an assembly line, promising mass consumption, but also a serious drop in quality.

Alternatives to force-feeding

The alternative to force-feeding, exploiting a natural ability of geese to overfeed and accumulate reserves before winter migration, is based on ad libitum feeding. It allows only one slaughter per year and the product obtained is marketed in England 60% more expensive than foie gras obtained by force-feeding. In France a team managed to produce foie gras without force-feeding by successfully selecting bacteria to optimize the corn ingested by animals. A dose of 0.3 ml of these ferments given to day-old goslings is sufficient to activate the natural phenomenon of fatty accumulation in the liver.

Several vegetable pâtés are also presented as substitutes for foie gras. The Belgian association for the defense of animal rights GAIA has been marketing fake fat since 2009, presented as an alternative. It is a vegetable terrine of German manufacture, produced for a long time by the company Tartex, flavored with champagne and truffles. The product is the subject of careful communication aimed at the same luxury image as foie gras, and its orders have increased from 30,000 jars in 2009 to 185,000 in 2014. In France, there are several vegan recipes, such as "Tofoie Gras", made with tofu, invented by culinary author Sébastien Kardinal, or "Bonfaiti" by chef Marie-Sophie, a vegetable and raw terrine base of cashew nuts, mushrooms, miso, coconut oil and spices, now known as "false fat". Increasingly widespread, it has become a quality dish just as much as the original foie gras.

Contents

Foie gras: about	5
A few words about this series	*5*
Now about the foie gras	*6*
Its history	*7*
Alternatives to force-feeding	*8*
Foie gras: the recipes	13
1. Artichoke Bottoms, Bayard Style	*15*
2. Artichoke Bottoms, Colbert Fashion	*15*
3. Aspic de Foie Gras	*15*
4. Attereaux, Villeroi Style	*16*
5. Ballettes Of Foie Gras à L'Imperiale	*17*
6. Ballotines Of Duckling, Freneuse Style	*17*
7. Boned Capon, Stuffed, Banker's Fashion	*18*
8. Boudin Of Chicken, Lucullus Style	*19*
9. Breasts Of Chicken, Opera Style	*20*
10. Brown Purée For Egyptian Cream	*20*
11. Buttered Eggs	*20*
12. Canapé MonteCarlo	*26*
13. Capon Souffled	*26*
14. Capon, Derby Fashion	*27*
15. Chaud froid Of Lamb Cutlets As Pears	*29*
16. Chaud froid Of Squab, Bohemian Fashion	*29*
17. Chaudfroid Of Chicken Legs As Ducklings	*31*
18. Chaudfroid of Reed birds	*32*
19. Chestnut Timbals, St. Hubert Style	*32*
20. Chicken à La Savoy	*33*
21. Chicken, Turtle Fashion	*34*
22. Chickens à La Chanceliere	*35*
23. Cold pies and how to make them	*36*
24. Cold Turkey à La Grande Duchesse	*36*
25. Consommé, Infanta Style	*38*
26. Cotelettes De Pigeon à La DUxelles	*38*
27. Cream Mixture à La Montreal	*41*
28. Cream Of Rabbit à La Duxelle	*42*

29. Crème De Lapereau à la Reine	42
30. Crepinettes à La Belgrave	43
31. Crepinettes à la D'Estine	44
32. Crepinettes à la Favorite	45
33. Croustade à la Champenoise	45
34. Croustade of Larks	47
35. Eggs à l'imperatrice	47
36. Eggs À la belmont	48
37. Eggs à la Belmont	49
38. Eggs à La Commodore	49
39. Eggs à la livingstone	50
40. Eggs à la Mme Morton	50
41. Eggs Benoit	51
42. Eggs Chateaubriand	51
43. Eggs Cocotte, Hackett	51
44. Eggs Epicurienne	52
45. Eggs gourmet	52
46. Eggs Henri IV	52
47. Eggs mirabeau	52
48. Eggs Mirabel	52
49. Eggs Talleyrand	53
50. Eggs Troubadour	53
51. Eggs, Balfour	53
52. Eggs, Strasbourgeoise	53
53. Eggs, Waterloo	54
54. Escalopes Of Pigeons à La Lisbonne	54
55. Farce For Chicken à La Chanceliere	55
56. Farce For Cold Pigeons, Partridge, Etc	56
57. Farce For Larks à La Sotterville	56
58. Farce For Pigeons Farced With Truffles	56
59. Farce For Turban à La Piemontaise	57
60. Fat Goose Liver Collops, Diplomat Style	57
61. Musslin of Fat Goose Liver, Bohemian Fashion	58
62. Fat Goose Liver Medallions, Aiglon Style	58
63. Filet mignon, Bayard	58
64. Filet Mignons, Belmont	59
65. Filet Mignons, Bennett	59
66. Filets De Boeuf à la Raifort Aux Oeufs	60
67. Filets de Poulet à la Strasbourgienne	65
68. Foie Gras à La Chateau Doré	66
69. Game Force meat	67
70. Game Pie	67
71. Garnish à la financière	68
72. Garnish à la Toulouse	68

73. Imitation Paté De Foie Gras	69
74. Imitation Patés de Foie Gras	69
75. Kromeskys	70
76. Lamb Cutlets, Agnes Sorrel Style	71
77. Larks à La Reyniere	71
78. Little Bouches Of Foie Gras à La Russe	72
79. Little Cases à La Strasbourg	73
80. Little Chicken Creams à La Gastronome	74
81. Little Creams à La Pothuau	75
82. Little Fillets Of Beef à La Valais	76
83. Mignons Or Beef, Immaculé	77
84. Mousse Of Foie Gras à La Rossini	77
85. Mutton Chops, Maison D'Or	78
86. Nerac Terrine	78
87. Noisettes Of Lamb, Rothschild Style	80
88. Pain De Volaille Au Foie Gras	80
89. PatÉ de foie gras	80
90. Pâté de Foie Gras Canapés	81
91. Paté De Foie Gras In Aspic Jelly	82
92. Pheasant Pie à La Française	82
93. Pheasants à la bohèmienne	84
94. Pigeons en Poqueton	84
95. Plovers' Eggs In Aspic à La Victoria	84
96. Poached eggs, à la Reine	85
97. Poached eggs, gourmet	85
98. Poached eggs, Perigordine	86
99. Poached eggs, Talleyrand	86
100. Potato salad	86
101. Pullet à la Montmorency	87
102. Purée For Cutlets Of Quails à La Greville	87
103. Puree For Little Swans à La Phrygienne	87
104. Quails à La Lesseps	88
105. Ragout For Eggs In Chaudfroid	89
106. Ragout For Filling The Quails à La Lesseps	89
107. Ragout For Little Timbals à La Monaco	90
108. Ragout For Patties à La Montrose	90
109. Reed birds in Aspic	90
110. Rillettes de Tours	91
111. Salmi of Larks à la Macédoine, cold	91
112. Salmis of Snipe	92
113. Sandwiches à La Fiane	93
114. Savory forcemeat	93
115. Scrambled Eggs, Schmidt	94
116. Skewers Of Fat Goose Liver, Villeroi Style	94

117. Small cakes of potatoes	94
118. Small Snipe Patties, Epicurean Style	94
119. Small tenderloin steak, Rachel	95
120. Souffle Of Foie Gras à La Montreal	95
121. Squab Cutlets, Sylvia Style	96
122. Stuffed eggs, Epicure	96
123. Stuffed Pullet	97
124. Supreme De Volaille	98
125. Surprise Eggs In Nest	100
126. Sweetbread, Junot Style	100
127. Sweetbreads Victor Emmanuel	101
128. Terreen Of Partridges, Parisian Style	102
129. Terrine de foie gras à la gelée	102
130. Terrine de foie gras en aspic	103
131. Terrine Of Plover	103
132. Timbale of partridges	104
133. Timbals For Chicken à La Chancelière	105
134. Timbals Of Foie Gras à La Beatrice	105
135. Tournedos, Bayard	106
136. Tournedos, Cussy Style	106
137. Tournedos, Rossini	107
138. Vol Au Vent Financière	107
Index of sources	111

Foie gras: the recipes

1. ARTICHOKE BOTTOMS, BAYARD STYLE

Fill some cooked artichoke bottoms with purée of paté de **foie gras**, cover with chicken cream forcemeat, smooth the surface with a knife dipped in lukewarm water, and decorate to your fancy. Then range in a buttered sauté pan, moisten with broth about 1/2 inch high from the bottom, and cook for 10 to 15 minutes.

Shred fine I part each of truffles, mushrooms, smoked beef tongue and breast of chicken; heat in Madeira sauce, and pour on a dish.

Dress the artichokes over the garnishing.

2. ARTICHOKE BOTTOMS, COLBERT FASHION

Pick out some small cooked artichoke bottoms and lay in each some purée of **foie gras**, place one bottom on top of the other (so that the purée is in between), stick a small wooden skewer through them to hold them together, dip in frying batter and fry in very hot lard. Remove the skewer and dress on a folded napkin with fried parsley.

Serve Colbert sauce separate.

3. ASPIC DE FOIE GRAS

Heat three pints of consommé, to which add three ounces of gelatine, a branch of tarragon, a tablespoonful of tarragon vinegar, and two wineglasses of Madeira (or sherry). Simmer gently, and, when your gelatine is dissolved, remove your saucepan to the side of the range.

Mix the whites of four eggs with a glass of cold water, and add them to your jelly, also the juice of a lemon; stir until thoroughly mixed. Simmer gently at the side of the range for half an hour, then strain through a flannel several times, or until perfectly clear. Take a round mold with a hole in the middle, place it on the top of some cracked ice, and pour in the bottom a few tablespoonfuls of jelly. When stiff, decorate it with truffles and the whites of hard-boiled eggs, cut in any fancy form which pleases you, then put on top another layer of jelly, let it stiffen, then add a layer of pâté de **foie gras** cut in pieces, then another layer of jelly, and so on, in the same manner, until your mold is filled, then put it on the ice for an hour. Then turn out your jelly on a dish, and put in the middle a sauce remoulade, or sauce ravigote, or sauce tartare. Instead of pâté de **foie gras**, slices of cold chicken, turkey, sweetbreads, or lobster may be used.

The receipt for this jelly is given as it is generally made in this country, where gelatine is much used.

4. ATTEREAUX, VILLEROI STYLE

Cut some 1/4-inch thick slices of **foie gras**, truffles, mushrooms and smoked beef tongue; scoop them out round and all of the same size; stick them alternately on to a skewer; spread over some Villeroi sauce, and lay on an oiled dish to get firm; egg and bread-crumb, and fry them in hot lard. Serve on a napkin and garnish with fried parsley.

5. BALLETTES OF FOIE GRAS À L'IMPERIALE

Line some ballette moulds thinly with aspic jelly, and garnish them with egg mixtures, in red and white, stamped out into tiny rings the size of a threepenny piece; set this garnish with a little aspic jelly, and then till up the centres with a nice piece of paté de **foie gras**; set this with more liquid aspic jelly, close up the moulds and leave them till the contents are firm.. Then dip each mould into hot water, and turn out the ballettes on to a bed of finely-chopped aspic jelly; garnish with sprigs of tarragon and chervil, and halves of cooked artichoke bottoms that are filled with flageolets mixed with a little salad oil, tarragon, and chilli vinegar, and serve for an entree for dinner or luncheon, or any cold service.

6. BALLOTINES OF DUCKLING, FRENEUSE STYLE

Take the skin off a duckling, divide it in eight equal parts. Bone the bird completely, keeping the breast for further use.

Free the remainder of the flesh from bones and sinews, add the same amount of breast of fowl and half of fat pork; chop fine and pound in the mortar, adding one-fourth the amount of bread crumbs soaked in milk, a tablespoonful of cooked force-meat and 1 whole egg; season with salt and allspice. Cut the breast in small squares, and sauté them in butter just long enough to stiffen them; drain, and when cold add the forcemeat with the same amount of **foie gras** cut in squares.

Spread the skin of the duckling on the table, divide the force-meat in as many parts as there are pieces of skin, wrap them up first with the skin and then with a clean, white cloth, and cook them for 30 minutes in the stock prepared with the bones.

Meantime, peel as many large white turnips as there are ballotines, cut them straight at the bottom and scoop them out at the top to make them hold the ballotines; parboil he turnips in salted water for 5 minutes, then drain.

Set the ballotines in the turnips, and place these in a sauté pan; moisten with the stock of the duckling, and cook for about 20 minutes longer, glazing the duck at last.

Dish up the ballotines, reduce the stock in which they were cooked, and finish with brown sauce; pour part of it on the dish, and the rest serve separate.

7. Boned Capon, Stuffed, Banker's Fashion

Singe, draw and bone a Philadelphia capon, laying aside the drumsticks. Prepare a force-meat with 1 pound each of turkey breast, lean pork and fat pork, to which add 1/2 pound of bread crumbs soaked in milk. Chop and pound the meat very fine, season with allspice, pepper, salt, a half pony of brandy and one of sherry, and some truffle juice. Cut into 1/2-inch squares 4 ounces of smoked beef tongue, 1/2 pound of truffles and 1 pound of fat goose liver (**foie gras** au naturel); mix these ingredients with the forcemeat, fill up the capon, and sew the bird together, trying to give it as much as possible its natural shape.

Line the bottom of a braising pan with a few slices of raw ham, 3 or 4 sliced carrots, 1/2 dozen sliced onions, a few parsley roots, 2 bay leaves, a sprig of thyme, and 1 dozen pepper corns; lay the capon thereon, surround with a few broken veal bones, set on the range, and after the vegetables are slightly browned, moisten with half veal stock and half consommé; cover tightly and cook in the oven for 2 1/2 hours, basting the capon every once in a while.

When done, strain the gravy, add a pinch of sugar and thicken with cornstarch diluted with a little sherry.

8. BOUDIN OF CHICKEN, LUCULLUS STYLE

Prepare some chicken forcemeat and keep it rather firm. Chop fine 1 onion, and fry it colorless in butter; drain and add it to the forcemeat; also add a quarter of its amount equal parts each of truffles, mushrooms and **foie gras** cut in very small squares; take a tablespoonful of this preparation at the time and lay it on a floured marble or table. Shape into flat oval rounds, lay them on a buttered pan and cover with boiling salted water; set on the fire and remove at first boil; allow to stand on the corner of the range for 10 minutes, then withdraw and allow to get cold.

Drain and dry the boudins, egg and breadcrumb them, and fry in hot lard. Serve on a napkin with Perigueux sauce separate.

9. Breasts Of Chicken, Opera Style

Prepare breasts of chicken as described for à la Florian[1], but instead of dipping them in melted butter dip them in beaten eggs and bread crumbs, and fry in clarified butter.

Serve the following sauce separate:

Opera Sauce. - Pound in the mortar 2 ounces of fat goose liver (**foie gras**) with 2 ounces of sweet butter and rub through a fine sieve. Heat I pint of cream sauce, add to it 2 tablespoonfuls of beef extract and finish with the goose liver butter; season with salt and paprika.

10. Brown Purée For Egyptian Cream

Rub three ounces of paté de **foie gras** through a fine hair sieve, and mix with it some of the chicken stock in which a tablespoonful of stiff Brown sauce has been mixed, then add cream and use.

11. Buttered Eggs

Buttered Eggs (*oeufs brouillés*) are undeniably good if served quite simply, upon crisply fried bread, straight from the fire. Grated ham, finely minced tongue, and little dice of crisply fried bacon, are capital, if at hand, to garnish

---

[1] [*Breast Of Chicken, Florian Fashion*: Lift the breasts from as many chickens as are needed, leaving the wing-bone on; remove the surrounding meat from the latter, and the epidermis from the breast; season, dip in melted butter, and then in bread crumbs, mixed with one-third of finely chopped ham; broil over a clear fire and serve with pepper sauce.].

the surface of the eggs with; and chopped herbs, anchovy, or the minced remnants of any fish like sardines, pilchards, or herrings, may be stirred into the eggs just before serving with marked advantage. Cold cooked vegetables, such as cauliflower, artichokes, asparagus, etc., may be cut up and mixed with the eggs in the same way, - in fact, a moment's thought will generally enable a careful cook to make his buttered egg toasts additionally tasty by the introduction of some nice trifle left from a previous meal, which could scarcely be made use of in any other manner.

Hard-boiled eggs make a very eatable toast in this way:- Grate a coffee-cupful of corned beef, bacon-lean, or ham; cut four hard-boiled eggs into eight pieces each; mix a good sauce blanche rather thickly, flavour it with a teaspoonful of anchovy sauce, and slip into it, so as to get thoroughly hot, the cut up eggs; when steaming, pour the contents of your sauce-pan over four nicely fried squares of bread, dust the grated beef over their surfaces and serve at once.

The happy owners of dairies to whom cream is not an extraordinary luxury should try:-

"Roties des oeufs à la crème" which are simply poached eggs served upon crisply fried toasts, with thick boiling cream poured over them.

Woodcock toast is one of the most recherché of all savoury entremets of this class. Numerous recipes are given for it, and its name is distorted by many writers upon cookery, some of whom present it to their readers under the meaningless title of "Scotch-Woodcock." In its unpretending form this toast is exceedingly like one I have already given, viz.:- a better kind of anchovy toast with an egg-cream custard top-dressing, but real "Woodcock-toast" should be composed as follows:-

Take two freshly boiled fowl's livers, - /those of a goose, a turkey, or a couple of ducks, are better still, while the remains of a paté de **foie gras** are superlatively the best) - pound the liver to a paste, mixing with it a tea-spoonful of anchovy sauce, or the flesh of one fish pounded, a pinch of sugar, plenty of fresh butter, and the yolk of one raw egg; dust into it a little spiced pepper, pass it through the sieve, and set it aside on a clean plate. Prepare four squares of golden-tinted, crisply-fried, bread, about half an inch thick, spread the liver paste over them and set them in a moderate oven to retain their heat, but not to burn. Now, pour a coffee-cupful of good cream into a sauce-pan, which must either be dipped into a bain-marie, or placed over a very low fire indeed; stir into it, as it warms, the carefully strained yolks of two raw eggs, continue stirring one way till the cream thickens nicely and is quite hot (without boiling) and pour it over your toasts: the egg whites (whisked by an assistant to a stiff froth whilst you were heating and thickening the cream) should be laid on the top of all, and the dish sent up without delay.

Or the preparation may be slightly varied as follows:- Fry the toasts, butter them, and set them in a moderate oven to keep hot. When heating the cream, stir into it the liver-paste as well as the raw yolks of two eggs, and pour it over the toasts as soon as it is quite hot, and thickened sufficiently, capping your dish with the whisked whites.

Kidney toast is generally far from being considered a very dainty one. Let me suggest two methods, one with the kidneys au naturel, the other made with those which you can cut out of a cold roast saddle:-

(a) - Take four ordinary kidneys, and blanch them first of all in scalding water then lift them out, and dry them in a cloth. Make a strong broth or gravy out of any bones or scraps you may have, and stew the kidneys therein till they are nice and tender, then take them out, drain them, and pour the gravy in which they were cooked into a bowl. Now, cut up and pound the kidneys to a paste in your mortar with some butter, and pass it through your sieve. When ready, skim any grease that may have risen to the top of your gravy, and take a medium-sized sauce-pan, working as follows:- Melt a dessert-spoonful of butter at the bottom of the sauce-pan, stir into it a dessert-spoonful of flour, when creamy, add by degrees a breakfast-cupful of the gravy and lastly, kidney-paste until all is expended: flavour the purée, with one table-spoonful port wine, one tea-spoonful red currant jelly, one dessert-spoonful anchovy vinegar, and a few drops of chilli vinegar. Let the contents of your sauce-pan thicken properly by coming to the boil, and then pour the purée over four squares of hot fried toast. Let there be no delay in serving. If made exactly in this way, this toast will be found an excellent one.

(b) - Cut the kidneys out of the cold saddle, together with all the fat belonging to them; chop up as much fat as there is of kidney meat for the toast, and throw the remaining fat, freed from all burnt skin, etc., into your frying-pan: now, fry in the melted fat a large round of bread till it turns a golden yellow, and has sucked up a good deal of the fat. Take it out, place it on a flat silver dish, cover its surface with the chopped pieces of kidney and the fat that you saved, pour the remaining melted fat over it, divide it into portions, and put it in the oven. When quite crisp, and 'short,' serve straightway without tear. Mustard, Nepaul pepper, and salt, should accompany, and hot plates should be placed before each guest.

Savoury toast made of the remains of cold roast game are delicious. Teal, wild-duck, snipe, quails, and florican; young pea-fowl, spur-fowl, jungle-fowl, and even partridges, may be thus presented a second time, forming a kind of rechauffe which rarely fails to be appreciated. The method of preparing a game-toast is somewhat similar to that 1 have described for "kidney toast" (a). The cold meat should be picked from the bones, and pounded with a Little butter to a paste: the skin and bones (well mashed) should be Bet to make a good, strong, game-flavoured gravy wherewith to form a thick purée in conjunction with the pounded meat. Pour the purée over hot fried toasts, and serve without hesitation.

All purées of game composed for toasts should be mixed rather thickly so as to rest upon the toast, and not spread all over the dish. Nepaul pepper, and quarters of limes, should be handed round with them.

I have already said that spinach, and other delicate greens - worked up in the form of purées - were very nice if served upon anchovy toast. They make capital toasts alone. A well made purée of spinach laid upon a crisply fried, and well buttered toast, is decidedly good; a poached egg, or a layer of "buttered eggs," can be added, of course, with additional effect.

An excellent toast can be made with the tender leaves and stalks of the beetroot. After having been boiled and drained like spinach, they should be chopped up and heated in a saucepan with some butter, salt and pepper, and spread upon hot fried toast with as little delay as possible. Country greens, the leaves of the mollay-keeray especially, and (with slight modification according to their peculiarities) nearly all vegetables can be dressed in this manner.

Vegetable marrows and cucumbers should be trimmed in neat fillets, their seeds should be cut out, and the pieces thus prepared should be boiled in hot salted water. These may be warmed again in a good sauce blanche or a nice thick brown sauce, laid upon toasts, and sent up. Or they may be heated up in boiling cream, and similarly served. The points of asparagus, cauliflower flowers, artichoke bottoms, and similar dainty vegetables, form admirable materials for toasts: they deserve delicate treatment, and can well bear association with thickened cream, velouté au Parmesan, or crème d'anchois.

12. CANAPÉ MONTECARLO

Puree of **foie gras** lightly mixed with a little stiff mayonnaise and spread on thin toast. Garnish around the edge with chopped yolks of hard-boiled eggs, and serve on napkins with parsley in branches.

13. CAPON SOUFFLED

Prepare a capon as indicated for Capon, Doria Fashion[2]. Fill it with the same ingredients, and cover it with the breast cut in neat slices; cover the breast with the following preparation, giving the capon its original shape, or at least trying to give it a pleasant, somewhat plump appearance.

Pound fine in the mortar 1 pound of breast of fowl, add 3 ounces of **foie gras** and the whites of 2 eggs; season with salt, pepper and nutmeg and rub through a fine sieve; set on ice, and incorporate 5 gills of thick cream, by degrees only; at last add the whipped whites of 2 eggs.

Set the capon in a saucepan in which it can be handled easily, moisten with enough chicken or veal stock to prevent scorching, set

---

[2] See the recipe immediately below.

on the fire, cover and cook in a slow oven for 30 to 40 minutes.

Dress on a bed of rice cooked in chicken stock, or on a support of hominy, and serve separately some velouté cream sauce.

14. Capon, Derby Fashion

Select a good-sized capon, singe and draw it by the front opening so as to leave the lower orifice as small as possible, which is imperative if success is desired.

This method of drawing poultry may not be quite as desirable so far as speed is concerned, but it is preferable when the bird is intended for stuffing.

After the capon is singed and all the feather stumps are removed, make an incision on the back of the neck, cut the neck as near to the body as possible, and remove the pouch, being careful not to injure the skin. Introduce the index or middle finger in the aperture, detaching the lungs on both sides of the back of the bird. Next cut out the ring on the back orifice, and with the index finger detach the fat adhering to the rump.

Introduce through the front aperture the handle of a small kitchen ladle, which must be provided with a hook; place the hook behind the gizzard and gently draw out the intestines of the bird, being careful not to burst the gall.

With a little practice the operator will soon become familiar with this method.

Heat in a saucepan 2 ounces of butter; add to it 4 ounces of rice, stirring it for 3 or 4 minutes;

moisten with 1 quart of chicken broth. When boiling, add 1 onion stuck with 2 cloves; cover and set in the oven to cook for 20 minutes; then remove the onion and add 2 tablespoonfuls of chicken glaze, stir with a kitchen fork, and take from the fire.

Cut into 1/2-inch squares 4 ounces of fat goose liver (**foie gras**) and 3 ounces of peeled truffles; mix with the rice, season to taste and fill up the capon with this preparation. When stuffed sew up the openings, truss it to a nice shape, and cover with slices of larding pork.

Butter a braising pan, and line it with 2 carrots and 2 onions cut in slices; lay the capon thereon, add a faggot of herbs and a knuckle of veal cut in pieces; cover the pan, let it stand over a slow fire for 20 minutes, turning the capon every once in a while from side to side; then moisten with 2 gills of Madeira and 1 1/2 quarts of brown veal stock. Cover the pan and put it in the oven, basting the capon frequently. Cook the capon from 1 hour and 45 minutes to 2 hours, according to size.

The capon may be dressed on a support of hominy, which should be fancifully carved; surround with large truffles heated in the gravy of the capon.

Strain the gravy, remove the fat, and if too liquid, thicken with a little cornstarch or arrowroot.

Serve gravy separate.

15. CHAUD FROID OF LAMB CUTLETS AS PEARS

Choose some fine lamb cutlets from the first ribs only, trim them well and split them horizontally from the back. Fill them with the same forcemeat as used for Squab Chaudfroid, Bohemian Fashion[3]. Use a good quantity of stuffing, so that the cutlets will look like pears, wrap up the chops in thin slices of larding pork, tie them with a string and braise them with good stock, in which allow them to grow cold. When they are cold, drain and dry.

Mix some purée of **foie gras** or some waste **foie gras** paring with the same amount of butter. Spread this preparation over the cutlets to give them a smooth appearance and a resemblance to a pear, then set on ice.

Coat the cutlets with green Chaudfroid sauce and when set pour over cold melted aspic jelly.

Set the pears on a dish with the bone upward (so as to represent the stem of the pear) and serve.

16. CHAUD FROID OF SQUAB, BOHEMIAN FASHION

Bone 12 squabs, and cut them lengthwise in halves. Keep the bones and carcasses to flavor the sauce.

Prepare 2 pounds of chicken forcemeat, add to it 1/4 pound of cooked forcemeat, and season highly to taste.

---

[3] See *Chaud froid Of Squab, Bohemian Fashion*

Cut into 1/4-inch squares 6 ounces each of truffles, smoked beef tongue and fat goose liver (**foie gras**); add these ingredients to the forcemeat, and fill each half of squab with enough force-meat to give it nearly its original size.

Tie each bird in a small cloth, giving it a round, oval shape (like a boned turkey); place them in a saucepan with the bones, moisten with good stock, and let simmer for 20 to 25 minutes. Allow the birds to get hike warm, then put them under light pressure, and let them get cold. Strain the broth, reduce it to 2 gills and incorporate into it 1 1/2 pints of brown sauce; reduce it for 5 minutes, add 1 pint of meat jelly; reduce the whole to obtain 1 quart of sauce; strain and put away to get cold.

Remove the cloth from the squabs, trim them nicely (taking off all the skin), and then coat them with the sauce described above.

Decorate to your fancy with truffles, smoked beef tongue, white of hard-boiled egg, etc.; brush over with melted meat jelly, and when cold, arrange artistically on a dish.

17. CHAUDFROID OF CHICKEN LEGS AS DUCKLINGS

Proceed as in the previous receipt[4], adding small cubes of **foie gras**, ham and truffles to the forcemeat instead of cooked fine herbs; when the chicken legs are cooked and cold, cover them with chaudfroid sauce, the body brown and the bills yellow; imitate the eye with the white of hard-boiled egg and truffle, brush over with partly melted jelly and serve with salad.

---

[4] [«*Chicken Legs As Ducklings*: Braise the legs with vegetables and a good stock, and finish the gravy as indicated for other braised meats. Garnish according to taste. Leave on the chicken legs part of the thigh bone; remove the second joint bone and two-thirds of the drum-stick bone; stuff the legs with the same forcemeat as indicated in the previous receipt {see below, Chicken Legs, Stuffed}. Truss the legs to form small ducklings, the part of the thigh bone to form the bill, the drum-stick the neck, and the second joint the body. Braise as explained previously, and serve on a bed of noodles tossed in butter. The noodles represent the nest.»

«*Chicken Legs, Stuffed*: When preparing breasts of chicken for a dinner party or banquet there are the legs to be made use of. Leave on them as much of the skin as possible when taking the breasts from the chicken; take out the second joint bone and stuff the legs with chicken forcemeat mixed with cooked fine herbs and some chopped chicken livers; fold the skin over the stuffing and sew it up.»

18. Chaudfroid of Reed birds

Prepare as in last recipe[5] with *pâté de **foie gras*** force-meat. Butter a dozen dariole moulds. Put a bird in each, breast downward; put the dariole moulds in a pan with a little water, and set it in the oven for fifteen minutes; when cold, turn out the birds, wipe them, dip each in brown *chaudfroid* sauce, and put them on a dish to cool. When cold, lay them in rows against a pile of chopped aspic.

Brown Chaudfroid Sauce is made by putting a pint of Spanish sauce, a gill of cream, half a pint of aspic jelly together, and boiling them until they are reduced one quarter. Skim constantly, and strain for use.

White Chaudfroid Sauce is simply béchamel and aspic treated in the same way. It differs, of course, from plain béchamel in having the piquant flavor of the aspic; in appearance there is little difference.

19. Chestnut Timbals, St. Hubert Style

To a pint of purée of chestnuts add 3 raw egg yolks; butter some timbal moulds and line them with the purée about 1/2 inch thick, and fill the hollow with purée of game, either grouse or partridge.

Place The Timbals In A Pan With Water And Cook In A Moderate Oven For 15 Minutes; Dish Up And Serve With Madeira Sauce.

---

[5] See *Reed birds in Aspic*

20. Chicken à la Savoy

Pick, cleanse and singe a nice fat white poularde, and truss it for braising; lard the breast with fat bacon, and place the bird in a well-buttered stewpan and braise with vegetables, etc, as for 'Chicken with Nouilles'; cover the bird with a well-buttered paper, place the lid on the pan and fry for about twenty-five minutes, then add half a pint of champagne and the same of sherry, boil up and cook in a quick oven for about fifty minutes, occasionally basting the poularde over the paper and adding more of the wine as that in the pan reduces; then take up the bird and brush it over with warm glaze; strain off the liquor and add to it one ounce of glaze, the contents of a tin or large bottle of truffles, the juice of two lemons, a pinch of castor sugar, a dust of cayenne and a pint of reduced Espagnole sauce ; boil this up, then put the fowl in the pan, keep the gravy skimmed and let the contents boil for about fifteen minutes, then take up the bird, remove the strings, pour the sauce all over it, and garnish with large slices of goose liver (**foie gras** naturel) and hatelet skewers. The poularde can be boned if liked and filled with truffles and whole liver before braising. The preserved liver only requires to be heated before using, and this is done by placing the tin containing it in the bain-marie after it has been opened. Fresh truffles would be best if in season.

21. CHICKEN, TURTLE FASHION

This requires a pullet or young hen about six months old. Bone the bird; stuff with a forcemeat made of four parts minced veal, two parts chopped hard eggs, a half part lean boiled ham, two parts mushrooms, and two parts *pâté de foie gras*. First make the veal and ham hot in a little butter, then add the mushrooms and *foie gras*; moisten with stock or mushroom liquor, and *gently simmer* five minutes. Stir in two beaten yolks of eggs and a teaspoonful of lemon juice. Season with a saltspoonful of salt, a quarter one of white pepper, and a tiny pinch of nutmeg, grated. Stuff the fowl with this mixture; sew it up with trussing-needle and string; turn the skin of the neck half over the head, and cut off part of the comb, which gives the appearance of the turtle's head. Scald and skin four chickens' feet; cut off the claws, and insert two where the wings ought to be and two in the thighs, so as to look like turtles' feet. Put in a stewpan a tablespoonful of chopped boiled ham, an onion, and a small carrot cut up, with a tablespoonful of butter; let them brown very slightly, add half a pint of stock, skim it, lay the fowl in this stock, and stew gently for an hour and a half to two hours, or even longer, according to size. When quite tender take up the fowl, cut and remove the string with which it is sewn, lay it on its back on a dish, garnish the breast with sliced truffles cut in fancy shapes, place a crawfish tail to represent the turtle's tail. When eaten hot serve velouté sauce. This is an excellent dish cold garnished with aspic.

22. CHICKENS À LA CHANCELIERE

Take two good fat poulardes, bone them, free the feet from the top skin, and clip the nails off, and press them into the leg where the bone has been taken from; fill the birds with farce, and truss them for boiling, making them as nice a shape as possible; place a piece of fat bacon on the breast of each, and tie them up in a well-buttered cloth. Put into a stewpan the bones from the birds, the liquor and beards from the oysters used in the preparation of the farce, some vegetables, such as carrots, onions, celery, leek, thyme, parsley, and bayleaf, two blades of mace, a little salt, and a teaspoonful of peppercorns; place the poulardes on this, and cover with light stock or water; put the pan on the stove, just bring the contents to the boil, skim it, and let it simmer very slowly for about one and a quarter to one and a half hours. Take up, put away till cold, then remove the cloths and bacon, and mask one side of each poularde with Tongue purée, and the other side with Aspic cream. Take some prettily-cut shapes of truffle, and ornament the breasts of the birds with them, using a little liquid aspic jelly to keep the garnish in its place; then coat over the truffle with a little more of the jelly to give it a glazed appearance. Place in the centre of the dish on which the poulardes are to be served a block of boiled rice and some finely-chopped aspic jelly; arrange the poulardes as shown in the engraving; place a hatelet skewer in the centre of the rice, garnish the back and front of the rice block with Financiere garnish, and arrange round the base of the dish some tomatoes and little timbals of paté de **foie gras**, and serve for a ball supper or luncheon dish. The stock left from the braising of the poulardes will make excellent soup.

23. Cold Pies and How to Make Them

There are a variety of cold pies, such as veal and ham, chicken, fish, game, or **foie gras**. Line a mould with short paste and spread a thick layer of either meat, game, or fish forcemeat, fill up the mould with whatever meat or fish you intend using, press it down firmly, sprinkle with salt and pepper, and cover with a thick pie-crust; make a hole in the centre, put in a small roll of paper to keep it open, and glaze with whipped white and yolk of egg. Bake the pie, and when done, keep until cold. Fill up the hole in the paste with a lump of uncooked flour and water until time to serve.

24. Cold Turkey à La Grande Duchesse

Pick, singe, and cleanse the turkey, and draw the sinews from the legs; cut off its head, and open it at the back of the neck and remove the backbone and breastbone as far as the leg joint, removing the entrails with the carcasse; then stuff it, sew it up, and truss it for boiling. The feet should be just dipped in boiling water, and then the outer skin removed, the sinews cut off, and the toes cut short, and the lower part of the leg with the foot replaced; tie the turkey up in a well-buttered cloth, and put it to boil for one and a half to two hours, according to size of the bird, in good stock with vegetables, such as carrot, onion, celery, and herbs (basil, marjoram, bayleaf, thyme and parsley), a few black and white peppercorns, six or eight cloves, and a blade or two of mace; let the stock come to the boil, then draw the pan to the side of the stove and let it simmer gently till cooked. Take up the turkey, remove the cloth, and let it get cold; it is best to boil the turkey the day before it is to be dished up. When cold remove the strings, and mask the bird over with white Chaudfroid sauce, putting on two or three coatings of the sauce until it is well masked; when the sauce is somewhat set lightly mask that over with aspic jelly which is not quite set, so as to give the surface a polish, and at once sprinkle over it some finely-shredded blanched pistachio nuts; when the aspic is set dish up the turkey and garnish it round with ornamentally cut pieces of aspic; take three hatelet skewers, and on them place some of the prepared crayfish or cooked prawns, and truffle, or Financiere garnish, and paté de **foie gras**, and arrange them on the breast of the turkey, as in the engraving, also garnish the breast with cockscombs or Financiere garnish and truffles. This dish can be served for any cold collation, ball supper, etc, and forms an important dish. Poularde may be prepared in a similar manner.

25. Consommé, Infanta Style

Prepare the same paste as described for Florentine Garnishing[6]. Put the paste in a pastry bag provided with a 3/8-inch tube; lay some small heaps of paste on a buttered baking sheet; brush over with beaten egg, and bake in a medium oven. When cold, make an incision on the side of the puffs and fill with a purée of **foie gras**; serve these puffs separate to a rich consommé.

26. Cotelettes De Pigeon à La DUxelles

Prepare the pigeons boning them and leaving just enough of the leg to form the bone of the cutlet; bat and trim this neatly into shape, then cover or "mask" each pretty thickly with a rather stiff d' Uxelles sauce, and when this has set a little, brush each cutlet over with egg and then fine breadcrumbs, and fry in plenty of hot fat till of a golden brown (about twelve to fifteen minutes) and serve with rich brown sauce, strongly flavoured with mushrooms, shallot, and tomatoes, with a dash of white wine and a

---

[6] « Put into a saucepan 1 gill of water with 1 ounce of butter and a pinch of salt; when boiling, add 2 ounces of flour and stir vigorously to get a smooth paste until it detaches from the pan; take from the range, and after 5 minutes mix with 2 eggs (one at a time) and 1 ounce of grated Parmesan cheese. When cold, put the paste into a pastry bag with a tube one-quarter of an inch in diameter, and press the contents of the bag slowly into a pan of slightly salted boiling water, let cook for 5 minutes without boiling, drain and put into the consommé.»

spoonful of capers added at the last, and a garnish of broiled mushrooms. If the pigeons are boned and coated with a liver or **foie gras** farce, fried, and served with tomato sauce they are called *à la moderne*; in short, pigeons may be cooked and served with any variety of sauce and garnish, for example à la milanaise, spread with a liver forcemeat (not **foie gras**) fried, and served on a bed of well cooked macaroni mixed with white sauce strongly flavoured with grated cheese, strips of ham, and truffles, with the cheese sauce round; or on a bed of tomato sauce and macaroni, with a demiglace poured round; or d la chipolata, with a rich espagnole and a chipolata garnish; or à la flamande, with a good strong brown gravy (not thickened sauce) and a garnish of stewed cabbage, and carrots, turnips, tiny onions, etc., first cooked, then tossed in enough butter with a tiny pinch of sugar, to glaze them; or à la Montglas, when the rest of the flesh carefully picked from the carcasses of the birds is made into a rich mince with stock (made with the bones of the pigeons and a little strong stock, flavoured like an espagnole sauce), into which you stir some sliced truffles; or if cut in half, without boning, the pigeons may be grilled and served on a bed of spinach with tartare, mayonnaise, Cazanova, or any other nice iced sauce, the cold sauce blending admirably with the fire-scorched broil.

Another way is to bone the birds, then by means of a bag and Forcing pipe to fill them back into shape with a farce (prepared like the border for supreme of chicken à l'ivoire) well flavoured with truffles and **foie gras**, fastened into shape with a buttered band of paper; then set the birds thus prepared on a well buttered tin, and cook in the oven for fifteen to eighteen minutes, keeping them well basted all the time; then halve them with a warm we knife, brush them over with white of egg that has been broken up, but not whisked to a stiff froth, wrap each cutlet in a strip of pork caul, again brush over with white of egg, roll in minced truffle, and set them in a buttered baking tin covered with a buttered paper, and cook in the oven for ten minutes, after which they are dished on a potato border, and served with a quenelle mixture, or a financiere garnish, in the centre, and any rich sauce such as Perigueux, Champagne, etc, round it. It must be remembered that all birds, such as quails, partridges, larks, etc. (not to mention hares and rabbits), can be cooked by these recipes, by the use of a little intelligence and good will on the cook's part.

For instance, the green plover so often seen in poulterer's shops make a delicious dish if the fillets are used as above described; or, again, the foreign game sent over from the continent frozen, lends itself particularly well to these recipes, as its rather strong flavour is obviated by the sauces which would be almost wicked used in connection with our own fresh and delicately flavoured game. By the way, few people appear to know how well grouse and mushrooms go together. Fillet the birds (using the rest of the body for a broil or grill in connection with tartare sauce), and cook in a well buttered tin, seasoned with a little salt and pepper, a few drops of sherry and a very little stock, under a buttered paper, in the oven from eight to twelve minutes according to the thickness of the fillets (in Scotland where birds are plentiful a side of the breast should be allotted to each guest, but where economy has to be studied, slice down the fillets), and dish them alternately with delicately-fried croutons strewed with a d'Uxelles mixture, on a bed of mushroom purée prepared thus: Chop fairly fine a pound of well wiped mushrooms, and let them draw down (cook slowly) at the side of the stove with 1½oz. of fresh butter for seven or eight minutes, then stir in two tablespoonfuls of freshly grated white bread crumbs, season with a little coralline pepper and salt, add a spoonful or so of good brown sauce, and use.

27. CREAM MIXTURE À LA MONTREAL

Whip one pint of double cream till perfectly stiff, then whip half a pint of consommé or good chicken stock of the consistence of jelly with half a pint of aspic till spongy, add this to the cream with a dust of coralline pepper and a pinch of salt; cut up the contents of a small tin of paté de **foie gras** into tiny dice shapes with a wet warm knife and mix with the other ingredients, add two or three chopped truffles, and put all into a forcing bag with a plain pipe, and use as directed above [see *Souffle Of Foie Gras à La Montreal*].

28. Cream Of Rabbit à La Duxelle

Take a rabbit mould, lay it open, and place it on crushed ice in a basin; line both sides with aspic jelly about one-eighth of an inch thick, and when this is set line them again with fawn-coloured Chaudfroid sauce; let this set, then fill up the two parts of the mould with a purée of rabbit as below, keeping the mould in motion whilst adding this, so that the mixture becomes well imbedded. Take the contents of a small jar of paté de **foie gras**, and with a hot wet knife cut it through into two pieces; place one piece in the centre of the purée in each side, then partly close the mould and pour into it the remaining part of the rabbit purée, which must be in a semi-liquid state, so as to join all the contents together; close up the mould firmly with the pegs and place it into some ice, and leave it for about half an hour, when it will be set. When ready to serve, dip the mould into hot water and turn out the rabbit, put in two glass eyes, dish it on a bed of finely-chopped aspic jelly, and garnish it round, as in engraving, with little timbals cooked halves of artichoke bottoms, that are seasoned with a little salad oil, tarragon, and chervil, and tarragon vinegar, and serve for an entree or any cold collation.

29. Crème De Lapereau à la Reine

Have ready a pound of delicate rabbit quenelle farce, butter a border mould either plain or fluted, or a timbale mould as you please, strew it generously with chopped truffles, and fill it with the quenelle mixture; steam it for half an hour, then turn it out and serve with a good velouté sauce. A portion of paté de **foie gras** truffé carefully mixed in with the quenelle farce as described above[7] adds greatly to the flavour of this dish.

30. Crepinettes à La Belgrave

Pound in a mortar till smooth one pound of raw rabbit, veal, or chicken which is free from skin and bone, a quarter-pound of fresh raw pork, bacon, or spiced beef; then rub the mixture through a wire sieve, and mix with it in a basin two ounces of paté de **foie gras** (that has also been passed through a sieve), add one

---

[7] [*Cream Of Hare à la Ferdinand*: Take three-quarters of a pound of cold cooked hare (that left from a previous meal will do for the purpose), pound it till quite smooth with a dessertspoonful of Bovril, a wineglassful of sherry, a half-pint of Supreme sauce, one gill of Brown sauce, and adust of Marshall's Coralline Pepper; dissolve a quarter-ounce of Marshall's gelatine in half a pint of aspic jelly, and add this to the other ingredients; rub the whole through a tammy, and use. Line a fancy mould with aspic jelly, ornament it with stamped-out rounds of Aspic cream and Tomato aspic and truffle; set the garnish with more jelly, then fill up the mould with the prepared purée; let it remain on ice till set. Dip the mould into hot water and turn out the cream on a dish; garnish round the cream with a cooked macedoine of vegetables (these are kept in bottles or tins), season with salad oil, tarragon, and chilli vinegar, and a little mignonette pepper and salt. Serve for an entree for dinner, etc.]

very finely-chopped eschalot, a little salt and mignonette pepper, and one and a half raw yolks of eggs; divide this into portions about the size of a very small egg, and roll each piece with the hand into cylinder shape, using a little flour for the purpose; then roll them into raw white of egg, and garnish each in any pretty design with cut truffle or cooked ham or tongue. Well wash some pork caul, dry it in a clean cloth, and cut it in little square pieces sufficiently large to cover a roll of meat; wrap each roll in the caul, and place them in a sauté pan in boiling clarified butter, and fry for about ten minutes over a moderate fire (or put in a quick oven with a greased paper over) till they are a pretty golden colour. Dish up on a border of spinach or mushroom purée, en couronne, and serve with Piquant sauce round the dish.

31. CREPINETTES À LA D'ESTINE

Take a pound of partridge quenelle farce and add to it about 6oz. of par-boiled fat bacon and 4oz. of truffles, both cut into small dice (or use tiny cubes of paté de **foie gras** truffé); mix with these a tablespoonful of espagnole sauce and the same of strong glaze prepared from the partridge bones, seasoning to taste with cayenne; mix this all well together, then take spoonfuls of this mixture into your well floured hands, and mould these into egg shapes, wrap each in a piece of caul, flatten slightly on both sides, dip them in clarified butter, and fry a light golden brown, drain well, dish them in a circle, pour round them a demi-glace of partridge stock, into which you have stirred half an ounce of fresh butter, and the juice of half a lemon, and serve very hot.

32. Crepinettes à la Favorite

Prepare some good rabbit quenelle farce, using espagnole instead of white sauce and some paté de **foie gras** truffé; have ready some pieces of caul and lay on each a tea-spoonful of the farce, place on this a tiny fillet of rabbit, seasoned with white pepper, a very little salt, and a d'Uxelle mixture; cover this again with the farce, smooth it in a dome shape with a hot wet knife, and wrap the caul all round them, trimming it neatly; dip these quenelles into fine breadcrumbs, next into well beaten whole egg, and then into bread again, pressing the crumbs neatly round them with the blade of the knife. A quarter of an hour before serving, broil them over a slow clear fire, and as soon as they are coloured on one side turn them lightly and finish cooking the other. Dish them neatly on a border of fried bread, filling the centre with cooked mushrooms and very small poached quenelles, pouring a rich game-flavoured espagnole sauce over the whole.

33. Croustade à la Champenoise

Prepare a bread croustade as described above[8], and keep it hot. Meantime prepare a

---

[8] «Cut a slice of bread straight off the loaf about 1½in. to 2in. thick, trim this neatly into shape either oblong, round, or square, then mark out a line from ¾in. to 1in.

ragout as follows; Three-parts cook a good slice of ham, then take it up and cut it into little dice; now return it to the pan with a cooked carrot, some mushrooms, and two truffles cut to match; toss these all in a little fresh butter, moistening it now and again with clear stock and a glass of champagne; let it reduce till fairly thick, then remove all fat, and stir into it the breast of a cold roast fowl, two well washed anchovies, some blanched gherkins and some parsley, all minced small, and let it heat without actually boiling, seasoning it to taste with salt, white pepper, and lemon juice; then pour it all into the crouton, garnishing the latter with little rolls of fried ham, and if at hand, some tiny chicken quenelles. If liked, sweetbread or paté de **foie gras** may be sliced down and added to this ragout, which is an excellent way of using up otherwise unproducible scraps left over from a dinner party.

Like many other dishes of the sort this croustade would be very expensive if all its contents had to be got ready for itself, but when made in

inside the outer rim all round, sinking the blade of the knife to two-thirds of the depth of the bread, and fry this bread in plenty of hot fat till of a golden brown; then drain it well, and remove the inner circle or square, trimming off all the underdone, greasy bread inside just as you did for the vol-au-vent, and set it and the cover in the oven to crisp, being careful it does not burn. Fill this with any ragout to taste exactly as you would a pastry case. These croustades can be made any size you please.»

this way of dainty scraps, it is really a case of what our grandmothers called "elegant economy." It is on care of this kind that the success and inexpensiveness of cooking depends. It is not only in knowing and obtaining the best things that a good housewife scores, but in knowing how to utilise to the best advantage the bits left over. Any remains of game, hash, fricassee, salmì, etc., can all be served in croustades, and also in patties.

34. CROUSTADE OF LARKS

Bone two dozen larks, season, and put into each a piece of pâté de **foie gras** (truffled). Roll the larks up into a ball, put them in a pudding basin, season them with salt and pepper, and pour three ounces of clarified butter over them, and bake in a hot oven for a quarter of an hour. Dish them in a fried bread croustade, made by cutting the crust from a stale loaf about eight inches long, which must be scooped out in the centre and fried in hot lard or butter till it is a good brown.

Drain it, and then place it in the centre of a dish, sticking it there with a little white of egg. Put it into the oven to get hot; then put the larks into it, and let it get cold. Garnish with truffles and aspic jelly.

35. EGGS À L'IMPERATRICE

Toast six slices of bread; butter them, put on top a thin slice of *paté de **foie gras***, and on top of this a hot poached egg. Baste with a little melted butter, dust with salt and pepper and send at once to the table. This is one of the most elegant of all the egg dishes.

36. Eggs à la Belmont

Place in a sautoire eight well washed sound mushrooms, with half an ounce of butter, on the hot range, squeezing in just one drop of lemon juice, let gently simmer for three minutes; add a sound finely sliced up truffle, also half a wine glass of Madeira wine; let reduce to one half, which will take about three minutes, add then a gill of Espagnole sauce and cook for three minutes longer.

Prepare twelve small paté de **foie gras** balls the size of a Malaga grape, gently dip them in beaten egg, then in fresh bread-crumbs, and then fry them in very hot fat for two minutes, or until they obtain a good golden color, remove them with a skimmer, and lay them on a napkin to drain.

Take up the mushrooms and truffles with a skimmer from the sauce, arrange them in two clusters, one at each end of the dish, as well as the twelve croquettes, also in clusters, six on each side of the dish.

Poach six very fresh eggs. Cut out from an American bread six round croûtons, arrange them on the hot dish all around. Plunge into hot broth or consommé six artichoke bottoms, take them up and place one on each croûton. Pour the sauce right in the middle of the dish, but not over the eggs; place a slice of truffle on top of each egg, and serve.

37. Eggs à la Belmont

Place in a sautoire eight well washed sound mushrooms, with half an ounce of butter, on the hot range, squeezing in just one drop of lemon juice, let gently simmer for three minutes; add a sound finely sliced up truffle, also half a wine glassful of Madeira wine; let reduce to one half, which will take about three minutes, add then a gill of Espagnole sauce and cook for three minutes longer.

Prepare twelve small paté de **foie gras** balls the size of a Malaga grape, gently dip them in beaten egg, then in fresh bread crumbs, and then fry them in very hot fat for two minutes, or until they obtain a good golden color, remove them with a skimmer,, and lay them on a napkin to drain. Take up the mushrooms and truffles with a skimmer from the sauce, arrange them in two clusters, one at each end of the dish, as well as the twelve croquettes, also in clusters, six on each side of the dish.

Poach six very fresh eggs. Cut out from an American bread six round croutons, arrange them on the hot dish all around. Plunge into hot broth or consommé six artichoke bottoms, take them up and place one on each crouton. Pour the sauce right in the middle of the dish, but not over the eggs; place a slice of truffle on top of each egg, and serve.

38. Eggs à la Commodore

Cut slices of bread in circular pieces and sauté in butter. Remove a portion of centre, leaving a rim one-fourth inch wide. Spread cavity thus made with pâté de **foie gras** purée, place a poached egg in each and pour over a rich brown or Béchamel sauce to which is added a few drops vinegar. Garnish with chopped truffles.

39. Eggs à la Livingstone
6 squares of toast
1 tureen of paté-de-**foie gras**
6 eggs
1/2 cupful of good stock
2 tablespoonfuls of sherry
1 teaspoonful of kitchen bouquet
1/2 teaspoonful of salt
1 dash of pepper

Toast the bread, butter it and put on top of each slice of toast a slice of *paté de* foie gras; put this on a heated dish, stand it at the mouth of the oven door while you poach the eggs. Put into a saucepan all the other ingredients, bring to a boil, put one poached egg on each slice of *paté de* foie gras; baste with the sauce and send at once to the table.

40. Eggs à la Mme Morton

Carefully crack six fresh eggs on a saucer; heat in a frying pan on the hot stove one tablespoonful of clarified butter, then drop in one egg and fry for two minutes, lift it up with a palette knife, carefully lay it on a hot dish, and continue the same with the other five.

Prepare six well designed round bread croutons. Lay a very thin slice, the size of the crouton, of paté de **foie gras** over each crouton, and then with a round paste cutter, two inches and a half in diameter, place it right in the centre of each egg, taking special care to keep the yolks exactly in the centre, so as to cut away the white of each egg evenly from all around each yolk. Place one egg on top of each crouton, pour a gill of hot Perigueux sauce, around the eggs, but not over them, and serve.

41. Eggs Benoit

Spread some paté de **foie gras** on four pieces of toast, lay a poached egg on top of each; and a head of fresh mushrooms sauté in butter on top of each egg. Cover with Madeira sauce.

42. Eggs Chateaubriand

Spread some **foie gras** on a piece of toast, lay a poached egg on top, and cover with tomato sauce.

43. Eggs Cocotte, Hackett

Open a small can paté de **foie gras**, dip a tablespoon in lukewarm water, then scoop out three tablespoons of the paté, discard all fat, then press through a sieve into a bowl and dilute with a gill and a half good cream. Season with two saltspoons salt, half saltspoon cayenne and half saltspoon grated nutmeg. Mix well, then divide evenly in six egg-cocotte dishes. Crack two fresh eggs into each dish. Evenly season with half teaspoon salt and two saltspoons pepper, place on a tin, then place in oven five minutes. Remove; finely chop one small truffle, place in a small frying pan with two tablespoons sherry, boil five minutes, then divide over the eggs in the six dishes and serve.

44. Eggs Epicurienne

Shir the eggs. When nearly done add a brown gravy to which has been added some small pieces of terrine de **foie gras**, four slices of truffle, and one sliced canned mushroom.

45. Eggs gourmet

Spread some terrine de **foie gras** on four pieces of toast, lay a poached egg on top of each piece, and cover with sauce Perigord.

46. Eggs Henri IV

Breaded poached eggs fried in swimming lard. Place on a piece of toast spread with purée de **foie gras**, and cover with sauce Perigordine.

47. Eggs mirabeau

Cut a sufficient number of rounds of bread, toast them carefully and cover them with *paté de foie gras*, put on top of each a poached egg, pour over sauce Perigueux, and send to the table.

48. Eggs Mirabel

Spread some **foie gras** on four pieces of toast, lay a poached egg on top of each piece, and cover with sauce Perigueux.

49. Eggs Talleyrand

Trim the bottoms of four fresh artichokes and put a little terrine de **foie gras** in each, and keep hot. Put a poached egg on top of each and cover with sauce Perigueux.

50. Eggs Troubadour

Spread four pieces of toast with purée de **foie gras** (goose liver paté), put a poached egg on top of each, and cover with sauce Perigord.

51. Eggs, Balfour

Cut off a third of six round rolls at the top, scoop out the soft parts, place them on a tin, then set them in the oven for two minutes, remove, then spread a teaspoon of paté de **foie gras** in the interior of each roll. Carefully crack six fresh eggs in two quarts boiling Water with two tablespoons vinegar and a teaspoon salt and boil for three minutes, lift them up with a skimmer and place an egg in each roll, dress the rolls on a hot dish, evenly pour a Bearnaise sauce over the eggs, arrange a thin slice of truffle on top of each egg and serve.

52. Eggs, Strasbourgeoise

Boil twelve fresh eggs for eight minutes, plunge in cold water for one minute, take up, shell, cut in quarters and keep on a plate. Skin four country sausages, place meat in mortar with a tablespoon paté de **foie gras** and pound to a pulp. Remove and divide the paste into hazelnut-sized balls, place in a sautoir with two tablespoons each sherry and demi-glace, then cook for five minutes. Add eggs with a half teaspoon each chopped parsley and salt, three saltspoons pepper, and gently mix. Cover sautoire, set in oven for ten minutes, remove, dress on a hot, deep dish and serve.

53. Eggs, Waterloo

Spread some **foie gras** on four pieces of toast, place a poached egg on each, and cover with Bearnaise sauce.

54. Escalopes Of Pigeons a La Lisbonne

Pick, singe, and bone a Bordeaux pigeon; then prepare a farce and spread it on the table; smooth it over with the hand, which should be occasionally dipped in cold water (as this makes the farce bind together and cut quite smooth and firm), and place in the centre of it some slices of paté de **foie gras**, and here and there little strips of truffle and cooked button mushrooms; roll up into a round form and place it in the pigeon. Lightly butter a piece of clean cloth, roll the bird in it, and tie it up tightly in the form of galantine. Put in a stewpan about three pints of boiling light stock, add the bones of the pigeon and one or two sliced peeled onions, one sliced carrot and turnip, a few strips of celery, a bunch of herbs, eight peppercorns, and two or three cloves; put the bird in the pan and allow the contents to simmer gently for about one hour; then take up the pigeon and retie it, and set it aside till cold. Then remove the cloth, and cut the pigeon into slices about a quarter of an inch thick; place these on a dish and mask them with Aspic cream ; let this set, then garnish with a little cut truffle, set this with a little liquid aspic, then trim and dish up on a block of aspic jelly; garnish with a macedoine of cooked vegetables that are strained and seasoned with a little salad oil, tarragon and chilli vinegar, and a little chopped tarragon; serve for an entree or second course, or any cold collation.

55. Farce For Chicken a La Chanceliere

Take, for two poulardes, four pounds of fresh fat and lean loin of pork, and free it from skin and sinews; also three pounds of fillet of veal, and three dozen bearded sauce oysters; pass these twice through the mincing machine or chop them very finely, then mix them in a basin with a half-pint of sherry, salt, and white pepper, the strained juice of two lemons, and three whole raw eggs; divide the mixture into portions, and place it on a well-wetted slab to about half an inch in depth, and make it quite smooth. Cut some very thin slices of French larding bacon, about nine or ten inches square and not quite a quarter of an inch thick; place these on the farce, and spread a layer of paté de **foie gras** all over it, about a quarter of an inch thick; sprinkle over this a little sherry and a little sliced truffle, pressing the latter well into the **foie gras**; then roll up the farce from the end in the form of a jam roll pudding, using a little cold water for the purpose, and use for stuffing any boned raw birds.

56. Farce For Cold Pigeons, Partridge, Etc

To farce one pigeon take six ounces of fresh pork or bacon and six ounces of white meat, and pound it till smooth, then pass it through a coarse wire sieve, season it with a little salt and white pepper; flatten the mixture out on to a wet slab, and place in the centre of it three ounces of paté de **foie gras** cut in strips, four good-sized truffles cut up, and two or three button mushrooms; roll up and use.

57. Farce For Larks A La Sotterville

Take, for twelve birds, six ounces of cooked pheasant or chicken, six raw bearded oysters and their liquor, two ounces of paté de **foie gras**, two tablespoonfuls of good Brown sauce, a teaspoonful of warm glaze, two ounces of panard, and two raw yolks of eggs; pound till smooth, season with a dust of Marshall's Coralline Pepper and a little salt, rub through a wire sieve, mix with two or three French red chillies that have been freed from seeds and cut up in little square pieces, put into a forcing bag with a plain pipe, and use.

58. Farce For Pigeons Farced With Truffles

Take half a pound of raw rabbit, a quarter of a pound of fat and lean loin of fresh pork, both weighed after being pounded and passed through a coarse wire sieve, mix with two raw yolks of eggs, a dust of Marshall's Coralline Pepper and a little salt, two ounces of paté de

foie gras, two ounces of fresh white bread-crumbs, half a wineglassful of sherry, mix well together, add a dozen large sliced truffles and use.

59. Farce For Turban a La Piemontaise

Pound four ounces of lean bacon or tongue, and ten ounces of raw chicken or other white meat, till smooth, and rub it through a wire sieve; then mix it with two ounces of paté de **foie gras** (that has also been rubbed through a sieve), and two large tablespoonfuls of thick Béchamel sauce ; season with a little white pepper and salt, and add two raw yolks of eggs, a tablespoonful of thick cream, and two or three finely-chopped cooked truffles or button mushrooms; stir these ingredients well together, put the mixture into a forcing bag with a large plain pipe, and use.

60. Fat Goose Liver Collops, Diplomat Style

Cut slices of cooked plain **foie gras** 3/8 inch in thickness; trim them all of the same size, cut the trimmings in small pieces, add the same amount of truffles and one-fourth the amount of well reduced German sauce. Cover the slices of **foie gras** on both sides with this mixture, and set on an oiled dish in a cool place.

When very cold, egg and bread-crumb the collops; fry in hot lard, serve on a napkin with fried parsley, and give Perigueux sauce separate.

61. Musslin of Fat Goose Liver, Bohemian Fashion

Pound fine 8 ounces of breast of fowl or turkey, then add the same amount of **foie gras** and 4 ounces of panada; add by degrees 3 egg yolks, and season with salt, pepper and nutmeg; rub through fine sieve and place in a cool place.

Work the forcemeat well in a bowl to make it smooth, and incorporate gently 1 pint of whipped cream; try its consistency; if too solid, add some more cream.

Butter some small timbale moulds, fill with some mousseline preparation, and cook in the bain-marie for 15 minutes.

Unmould, and dish up and pour over some cream paprika sauce.

62. Fat Goose Liver Medallions, Aiglon Style

Cut some slices of smoked beef tongue 1/4 inch in thickness, trim them all of the same size and shape (preferably an oblong round).

Cover one side with purée of **foie gras**, smooth over the surface and cover with white chaudfroid sauce; decorate the medallions with truffles, etc., brush over with partly set jelly, and dress on a border of aspic jelly.

63. Filet Mignon, Bayard

Sauté in butter, or broil, small tenderloin steaks, place on toast, spread with purée de **foie gras**, cover with sauce Madere with sliced truffles, and garnish with small round chicken croquettes.

64. FILET MIGNONS, BELMONT

Neatly trim a little fat off a two-pound piece tender filet of beef, then cut it in six equal pieces, season with a teaspoon salt and half teaspoon pepper. Thoroughly heat one tablespoon fresh butter in frying pan, arrange filets in one beside another and briskly cook for three minutes on each side Cut out from a sandwich loaf six slices a half-inch thick, cut in two-inch round pieces, lightly butter on both sides, place on a tin and set in oven for ten minutes or until a nice golden colour. Remove, spread a teaspoon paté de **foie gras** over each, arrange on a hot dish, place mignons on top of toasts, pour a Belmont sauce over and serve.

65. FILET MIGNONS, BENNETT

Remove skin and neatly trim a two-pound piece nice, tender filet of beef. Cut it in six equal pieces, season with a teaspoon salt, half teaspoon pepper, and keep on a plate until required. Peel, carefully wash and drain well twelve good-sized fresh mushrooms, place in a sautoire with a tablespoon melted butter, and gently cook for five minutes on each side. Sprinkle over a half teaspoon salt, squeeze in juice of a quarter of lemon, add two tablespoons sherry, shuffle well and keep them hot on range.

Prepare six round pieces toast, two inches in diameter and quarter of an inch thick, spread a teaspoon of paté de **foie gras** over each, then place on a hot dish.

Thoroughly heat a tablespoon melted butter in frying pan, place mignons in pan one beside another, and briskly cook for three minutes on each side. Dress them on top of toast, arrange two mushrooms over each mignon, pour Bennett sauce over all and serve very hot.

66. FILETS DE BOEUF A LA RAIFORT AUX OEUFS

Bat out and trim some neat round fillets, and broil these over a clear fire after brushing them over with oil or liquid butter; have ready some rounds of bread fried a delicate brown and brushed over with liquid glaze; also as many nicely poached eggs as you have fillets (mind these are nicely trimmed so as to have only a very tiny rim of white round them; indeed, many cooks use the yolk only for this purpose), then place a fillet of beef on each crouton, a poached egg on the beef and lastly a tiny heap of "Spring's horseradish cream "on top of all. Strictly speaking, any savoury butter can be used in this way, but this particular novelty is so very delicious it deserves special mention. Remember that when liquid glaze is mentioned, Liebig and Co.'s extract of beef is a particularly effective substitute for home-made glaze, always being at hand, and in good condition, which is more than can be said for the home-made glaze in every case. A small teaspoonful of this extract added to any sauce is an immense improvement, and will give strength and value to even second stock.

For the sauces a reduction it is particularly valuable.

Lastly, there are what may be classed as stuffed fillets, or filets fourres, i.e., when the piece of meat, of whatever shape you please (though usually a round form is preferred), is cut thick enough to allow of its being sliced (as for filets de boeuf aux huitres), any farce or stuffing being then introduced, as for example, à la St. James, when a slice of **foie gras** or liver farce is placed between the sides of the tiny steak, which is sauté, and finished off with a compote of cherries, and a rich mushroom sauce; or à la Grande Bretagne, when the meat is stuffed with a mixture of rather thick horseradish sauce, grated Parmesan cheese, and cooked macaroni cut into tiny rings, the fillets, when sautes, being served with fried potato straws, and a good brown sauce; or à la Riga, when a little delicate sausage meat is placed between the sliced meat, which is braised, and lastly served with brown sauce round, a garnish of sliced and broiled tomatoes, and a pile of peas, asparagus points, or any other nice vegetable in the centre; or à la Perigueux, i.e., stuffed with a ragout of truffles sliced and tossed in a little wine, sautes, and served with a rich tomato sauce.

In short, they may be varied almost ad infinitum, for if nicely sautes, or broiled, filets de boeuf may be served with almost any sauce, if care be taken as to the accompanying garnish, as, for instance, à la Nemours, i.e., stuffed with a delicate chicken forcemeat, and dished alternately with small slices of nicely broiled ham, and a rich allemande sauce. It may be mentioned that sometimes fillets of beef thus prepared are egged, breadcrumbed, and fried, the farce having been previously laid on the side of the fillet. (Cutlets are also very good served in this way.). Finally, there is the Chateaubriand steak, which was originally a piece of rump or fillet steak cut about 1½in. Thick and placed between two pieces of ordinary steak about ½in. thick, this being then broiled until the outside meat was all but a cinder, when it was. Served with the outer meat removed, and was found cooked just to perfection. This is, however, now simply an extra thick steak or filet, of which the outer sides are fairly scorched over a clear grill fire,. leaving the centre rather underdone and very juicy;. it is then served with a tiny ball of maitre d'hotel butter placed on a hot dish underneath it, a similar ball being placed on top of each filet, and a demi-glace thickened with maitre d'hotel butter being served round it, together with soufflé or straw potatoes.

The above will give some idea of the different ways of serving fillets of beef, whilst of veal it may be said that almost any recipe given for either mutton or beef cutlets or fillets will suit veal; the following, however, is the conventional "veal cutlet": Take either the "noisettes" from the best end of the neck, or a slice cut from the fillet about fin. thick, and shape this into rounds, batting these out neatly; either flour these well or dip them in egg and breadcrumb, in either case frying them in clarified butter till of a pale golden brown, and perfectly cooked (underdone white meat is unpardonable), which will take from twelve to fifteen minutes according to the size of the cutlets, then lift them on to a hot dish; meanwhile add a little more butter to that in the pan, dredge in about a dessertspoonful of fine dry flour and cook these together till of a very pale fawn shade (a spoonful or two of white wine may with advantage be added to this); now add gradually from a gill to one-third of a pint of good stock, or even boiling water, seasoning this to taste with pepper, salt, and lemon juice, boil it all up together, then pour it over and round the veal cutlets, which may be further garnished with slices of lemon and tiny rashers of bacon cooked thus: Slice the bacon very thinly, catting each rasher into two or three, roll each piece up neatly and thread it on to a skewer and toast or bake these lightly till just cooked.

Some people add the finely grated peel of a small lemon to the breadcrumbs in which the veal cutlets are rolled; or, again, you may add a dessert-spoonful of best curry powder to about 2oz. of breadcrumbs, and half a small teaspoonful of salt, and roll the egged cutlets in this; when fried, serve with good curry sauce.

It must be remembered that abroad veal cutlets are also cut precisely like mutton cutlets, from the best end of the neck, and treated in pretty much the same way; or they may be served au gratin (or à la bordelaise, as it is sometimes called) thus: Cut and trim the cutlets exactly as for mutton cutlets for egg and crumbing, and dust these well on both sides with salt and quatre epices, or pepper and a very little grated nutmeg; have ready a mixture made by mincing finely a good slice of bacon, a shallot, and a spray or two of parsley and tarragon, mixing this well with one raw egg, then spread a layer of this mince over each cutlet, and brush it over afterwards with the yolk of an egg; sprinkle a well buttered baking dish with finely grated bread crumbs seasoned with a little salt and white pepper, and lay in the cutlets side by side, moistening them with half a gill each of stock and of claret, and let them bake till cooked, which they will be, when the stock, Ac, is nearly all absorbed. Three well-known German dishes must be mentioned, as they belong to the fillet and cutlet genus.

The first is Wiener schnitzel.

For these cut the veal into rather thin fillets, rub these well with pepper and salt, and dip them into a good but rather light batter (or, if preferred, beaten egg yolk), then into crushed rusks (zwieback), and fry a golden brown in plenty of butter or lard. Serve well drained, sprinkled with a squeeze of lemon juice, and a garnish of fried eggs, capers, and filletted sardines arranged in a kind of trellis over all. Gulasch: Cut about a lb. of nice fillet of veal (free from all skin, sinew, etc.) into dice; cut up two small potatoes and one apple, washed and peeled in the same way, and mince down 4oz. of bacon. Melt 1½oz. fresh butter and fry in this half an onion finely minced, till slightly coloured, then lay in the minced veal, seasoning it with salt and pepper, and cook it gently for ten minutes over a clear fire (a hot oven will also do); now sprinkle it all with a dessert-spoonful of flour, moistening it with a gill of veal stock and half a gill of sherry or Madeira; add about a teaspoonful of carraway seeds tied up in a piece of muslin, and let it all simmer slowly together.

Meantime fry the minced bacon, potatoes, and apple slowly in 1½oz. of butter till of a pale golden brown, then pour off the fat, and stir the bacon, potatoes, etc., into the meat with a fork, being careful not to mash it as you do so. Let it all cook very gently together till the meat, etc., is thoroughly done, then lift out the carraway seeds, and serve very hot. This is an Hungarian dish, and the pepper used should be the Hungarian paprica. (Tender beefsteak is excellent also cooked thus.).

67. FILETS DE POULET À LA STRASBOURGIENNE

Roast two large fowls in vegetables, and when cold take out the fillets, and with a thin knife divide each fillet in halves, to form two out of one, then pound two ounces of **foie gras** de Strasbourg (a small tureen of which can be purchased at any respectable Italian warehouse in London) in a mortar, and rub it through a hair sieve, put a spoonful of chopped onions in a stewpan with half a pat of butter, stir them a few minutes over the fire, then add half a pint of white sauce, reduce till rather thick, add the **foie gras**, and when ready to boil take it off the fire and stir in the yolks of two eggs very quickly, leave it to get cold, then spread it over the fillets the eighth of an inch in thickness, have three eggs in a basin well-beaten, take each fillet on a fork, dip them into the eggs, throw them in a dish of bread-crumbs, take them out, pat them gently with a knife and repeat the operation, have four pounds of hot lard in a stewpan, in which fry them a light brown colour, dress in crown on a small border of mashed potatoes, and serve with fried water-cresses in the centre quite dry, with a little gravy separate.

68. FOIE GRAS A LA CHATEAU DORE

Take an opened tin of **foie gras** and stand it in the bain-marie till the contents are quite hot; then, when ready to serve, turn it out on to a plate and cut it into portions, and dish it up as in engraving on a border of chicken or rabbit farce with a small round of fried bread in the centre; garnish the **foie gras** with Financière that has been warmed in the bain-marie and with hatelet skewers; pour good Espagnole sauce round the dish, then place some cooked button mushrooms at each end of the dish and serve hot for an entree for dinner party.

69. GAME FORCE MEAT

One pound of game, 6 ounces of panada, 8 ounces of butter, 2 yolks and 3 whites of eggs and 3 gills of brown sauce well reduced, with essence of game prepared from the bones or carcasses.

When all these ingredients are well pounded, rub them through a fine sieve, put in a bowl, on ice, and incorporate 2 more gills of well reduced brown sauce. Season with salt, cayenne and nutmeg.

Farce a Gratin - Force-Meat Cooked. Fry 2 ounces of salt pork in 2 ounces of butter, add I small chopped onion and 2 shallots, a small sprig of thyme and I bay leaf.

Cut I pound of chicken livers in 3/4-inch pieces, and sauté them until well done; season with salt and pepper; pound in the mortar and rub through a fine sieve.

Note. - This forcemeat is usually mixed with other force-meats; it should be used judiciously; for matter of economy, or, if no chicken livers are on hand, calf's liver may be used, and on the other hand, if to be used for exceptional purposes, one-third part of fat goose liver (**foie gras**) may be added to the chicken livers.

70. GAME PIE

Take ten ounces of veal and the same of veal fat, and chop it very fine, season with pepper, salt, and cayenne. Arrange this as a lining round a china raised pie mould. Fill in with fillets of grouse, pheasant, partridge, and hare, strips of tongue, ham, hard-boiled yolks of eggs, button mushrooms, pistachio nuts, truffles, and pâté de **foie gras**; cover in with more of the mince, then put a paste on the top for cooking it in. Bake from two and a half to three hours. Remove the paste and fill the mould up with clarified meat jelly, partly cold; let this set.

Ornament the top with chopped aspic and alternate slices of lemon and cucumber round. Croûtons of red and yellow aspic should be arranged at the base of the mould.

71. Garnish à la financière

Cook some **foie gras**, cockscombs, and livers, chicken quenelles, mushrooms, and truffles in financière sauce, and use as a garnish.

72. Garnish à la Toulouse

This garnish is composed of scollops of **foie gras**, truffles, whole mushrooms, cockscombs, and livers, and lamb's sweetbreads. The scollops are made from previously cooked **foie gras**; the truffles must be boiled in glaze and white wine; the mushrooms blanched with butter and lemon juice; the cockscombs trimmed, washed, and boiled until they are blanched; the livers boiled, and the lamb's sweet-bread fried. All these ingredients are placed round the dish, the **foie gras** slightly glazed, the cockscombs, mushrooms, livers, and lamb's sweetbreads covered with velouté sauce, and the truffles strongly glazed.

73. Imitation Paté De Foie Gras

Wash and clean a calf's liver. Let it lie in salt and water for fifteen minutes. Boil till tender. Heat it through a coarse wire sieve. Add one tablespoonful melted butter. Season with a little thyme, marjoram, salt and pepper. Pack tight in pots. Cover with lard, and keep in a cool place. It will keep for several days.

To really imitate a paté de **foie gras**, this should have bits of tongue mixed through it, but it is just as good without.

74. Imitation Patés De Foie Gras

Boil a calf's liver until very tender in water that has been slightly salted, and in another vessel a nice calf's tongue. It is best to do this the day before you make your paté, as they should be not only cold, but firm when used. Cut the liver into bits, and rub these gradually to a smooth paste in a Wedgewood mortar, moistening, as you go on, with melted butter. Work into this paste, which should be quite soft, a quarter-teaspoonful of cayenne pepper, or twice the quantity of white or black, half a grated nutmeg, a little cloves, a teaspoonful of Worcestershire sauce, salt to taste, a full teaspoonful of made mustard, and a tablespoonful of boiling water, in which a minced onion has been steeped until the flavor is extracted. Work all together thoroughly, and pack in jelly-jars with air-tight covers, or, if you have them, in paté-jars. They give a foreign air to the compound, and aid imagination in deceiving the palate. Butter the inside of the jars well, and pack the paté very hard, inserting here and there square and triangular bits of the tongue, which should be pared and cut up for this purpose. These simulate the truffles imbedded in the genuine patés from Strasbourg. When the jar is packed, and smooth as marble on the surface, cover with melted butter. Let this harden, put on the lid, and set away in a cool place. In winter it will keep for weeks, and is very nice for luncheon or tea. Make into sandwiches, or set on in the jars, if they are neat and ornamental.

The resemblance in taste to the real paté de **foie gras** is remarkable, and the domestic article is popular with the lovers of that delicacy. Pigs' livers make a very fair paté. If you can procure the livers of several fowls and treat as above, substituting bits of the inside of the gizzard for truffles, you will find the result even more satisfactory.

75. KROMESKYS

Chop up some breast of chicken, fillets of partridge or pheasant, truffles, **foie gras**, pickled tongue, and mushrooms; warm in thick reduced Spanish sauce, and leave until cold.

Flatten out some calfs udders, lay a dessertspoonful of the forcemeat on each one, fold them over, dip into batter and plunge into boiling lard; when a good colour, drain the kromeskys, dish them up in a pyramid, and garnish with fried parsley.

76. Lamb Cutlets, Agnes Sorrel Style

Cut and trim some nice lamb cutlets, cook them lightly on both sides, and let them get cold.

In the meantime, prepare a forcemeat as follows: Chop fine 9 ounces of lean pork with 3 ounces of fat and 3 of **foie gras**; steep 3 ounces of soft bread in milk, press lightly and add to the forcemeat; pound in the mortar, season to taste with salt, pepper and allspice, and add a dash of brandy, 2 of Madeira and a tablespoonful of chopped truffles. Put some of the forcemeat on both sides of the lamb cutlets, wrap them in pig's caul, dip them in melted butter and bread crumbs, and broil over a slow charcoal fire. Serve with truffle sauce.

Note. - Instead of **foie gras**, chicken, turkey or calf's liver may be used.

77. Larks à la Reyniere

Take some boned larks and farce them with a little paté de **foie gras**, then put each in a small band of buttered paper and tie them up; butter a stewpan and put in it a slice or two of carrot, onion, turnip, leek, celery, a bunch of herbs, such as thyme, parsley, and bayleaf, and a few peppercorns; place the larks on these vegetables, put a buttered paper over them, and fry for about five minutes; add a quarter-pint of stock, place the pan in the oven for ten minutes, then take up the larks and remove the paper. Butter some little hexagon dariol moulds, sprinkle them with chopped truffle and then line them with beef farce, using a forcing bag and pipe for the purpose; make a little well in the centre of each with the finger, which should be occasionally dipped in hot water, place a lark in the space thus formed and cover over with more farce. Place a piece of paper in the bottom of a stewpan, on which put the dariols; pour in boiling water until it reaches to three-quarters the depth of the moulds, watch it reboil, then draw the pan to the side of the stove and poach for about fifteen minutes; turn out the dariols on to a border of farce, pour the sauce over them, and place the prepared heads and feet of the larks on the top of the portions, as in engraving, and serve for an entree for dinner. To cook the head and feet of the birds cleanse them, place them in a buttered paper, put to cook in the oven for ten to twelve minutes, and just before serving brush over with a little warm glaze.

78. Little Bouches Of Foie Gras à La Russe

Thinly line some little bouche moulds with aspic jelly, garnish them with little thinly-cut strips of hard-boiled white of egg, and place here and there, round the mould some little beads of the prepared red garnish, using a forcing bag with a small plain pipe for the purpose, and at the bottom of the mould form a little border all round with finely-shredded lettuce, setting it with a little more liquid aspic jelly. Place a little piece of paté de **foie gras** in the centre of each mould, then fill them up entirely with liquid aspic jelly, and put aside till set.

Take some little square paper cases, nearly fill them with the prepared salad, turn out the little bouches by dipping them in hot water and draining them on a clean cloth, and place one in each case on top of the green salad, and by means of a forcing bag with a medium-sized pipe form a little border of finely-chopped aspic jelly all round the edge of the case; place a tiny sprig of raw green chervil, or a small cleansed radish, at the four corners of each case, dish up on a dish-paper on entree or flat dish, and serve for cold entree, second-course dish, or for any cold collation.

79. Little Cases à la Strasbourg

Prepare about two ounces of savoury short paste, and with it very thinly line some little boat-shaped moulds; in each case put a little buttered paper to fit the mould, and fill it up with rice or dried grain, then put to bake in a moderate oven for about twenty minutes; remove the rice and papers, and put the cases back again in their tins in the oven to dry, if needed, till like biscuits. Take them out and let them get cool, trim them, take them out of the tins, and ornament the edges with fresh butter, using a bag with a small fancy pipe; lightly sprinkle over the butter a little finely chopped parsley, and fill the cases with a mixture of chopped olives, tongue, French gherkin, and apple, the latter seasoned with a little salad oil, chopped tarragon and chervil, and tarragon vinegar; on the centre of each cassolette place a little round of paté de **foie gras** stamped out with a plain round cutter. When required, serve each of them on a little plate or a little fancy saucer, and garnish with two little bunches of prettily shredded celery, which should be kept in cold water till wanted, then dried and mixed with a little chopped eschalot, tarragon vinegar, a little salad oil, and a tiny pinch of salt and use for a hors d'oeuvre. These can also be used as a savoury, in which case serve them on a dish in a pile.

80. Little Chicken Creams à la Gastronome

Take twelve ounces of raw tender chicken, free it from skin and bone and pound it till quite smooth, then add to it six ounces of pounded Panard, two tablespoonfuls of reduced Espagnole sauce, one ounce of butter, a pinch of coralline pepper, one tablespoonful of sherry, a little salt, and three whole raw eggs; mix well together, then rub through a fine wire sieve. Butter some peach moulds, and by means of a forcing bag and plain pipe nearly fill them with the prepared cream; form a little well in the centre of each by dipping the finger in hot water and working it round in the centre of the farce; place in the spaces thus formed one small whole or half a large truffle, a little piece of paté de **foie gras** about the size of a Spanish nut, and a saltspoonful of reduced consommé (that would be in a stiff jelly when cold); cover up the space with a little more of the farce, stand the moulds in a sauté pan on a fold of paper, place a buttered paper over the moulds, pour in sufficient boiling light stock to cover them, watch the stock reboil, then draw the pan to the side of the stove, cover the pan with the lid, and let the contents poach for about fifteen minutes; take up when firm, and set the creams aside till cold. Then turn them out of the moulds, mask them over with white Aspic cream till quite smooth and well coated, then glaze them over with a little cool liquid aspic jelly, and dish them up, as shown in the engraving, on a bed of finely-chopped aspic jelly. Arrange on the top of each cream a little ham purée, as below[9], using a forcing bag and small rose pipe for the purpose, and serve for an entree for dinner, ball supper, etc.

81. LITTLE CREAMS À LA POTHUAU

Take some little oblong sandwich moulds, line them very thinly with aspic jelly (that made with two and a half ounces of Marshall's gelatine to one quart of water), then ornament each with a little truffle cut in any pretty design; set this with a very little aspic jelly, then mask the moulds over with Chaudfroid sauce in alternate layers of red, white, and brown, and fill up the inside of the moulds with little

---

[9] «*Ham Puree For Chicken Creams A La Gastronome:* Take for eight to ten creams half a pound of lean cooked ham or tongue, two hard-boiled yolks of eggs, a few drops of carmine, a dust of coralline pepper, and a quarter-pound of fresh butter; pound altogether till quite smooth, rub through a fine wire sieve or tammy, and use as directed.»

stamped-out rounds of paté de **foie gras**, sliced truffle, mushroom, and chicken, arranging these overlapping each other; fill with some aspic jelly and put aside to get cool; then turn out the creams, by dipping the moulds into hot water, and dish them up on a border of aspic jelly or rice; garnish with salsifies (or other Dice cooked vegetables) in Tomato mayonnaise, over which sprinkle a few shreds of truffle. Serve for a cold entree for dinner, or for any cold collation. Take a small tin of paté de **foie gras**, for ten to twelve persons, turn it out on to a plate, remove all the fat, cut it in slices about a sixth of an inch thick, stamp it out in rounds the size of a sixpence, and serve for an entree for dinner or luncheon.

82. Little Fillets Of Beef à La Valais

Cut some very small round slices from the fillet of beef, bat them out with a knife, dipping it occasionally in cold water to prevent the meat sticking to it; then trim the fillets neatly, and season them with a little salt and pepper, and pique them with truffle and mushroom and bacon; place them in a well-buttered sauté pan and sauté them lightly on the under side for four or five minutes, then place them in the oven to finish cooking for the same time with a buttered paper over, then dish them up on a border of purée of mushrooms or any nice vegetables, such as a purée of spinach, etc.; place a little round piece of **foie gras** on the top of each fillet of beef, and on the **foie gras** a slice of truffle; serve round the base a good

Espagnole sauce, with two or three shredded truffles added when just about to serve. This can be served for dinner or luncheon.

83. MIGNONS OR BEEF, IMMACULÉ

Neatly trim a two-pound piece filet of beef, cut it in six even filets and season with a teaspoon salt and half teaspoon pepper. Thoroughly heat a tablespoon melted butter in frying pan, add the mignons, briskly cook for three minutes on each side, lift up and keep hot. Prepare six round toasts, two inches in diameter and half inch thick, butter on both sides, place on a tin and set in oven until a nice golden colour. Remove, spread a teaspoon paté de **foie gras** over each, dress on a hot dish, place mignons and spread evenly a Bearnaise sauce over them, place two thin strips truffles cross-like over all and serve.

84. MOUSSE OF FOIE GRAS A LA ROSSINI

Line a plain round Charlotte mould thinly with liquid aspic jelly, ornament it with truffles, gherkins, red chillies, and hard-boiled white of egg that are cut in slices 'then stamped out in any pretty designs, setting them to the mould with a little more aspic to keep them in their places. Take the contents of a jar of paté de **foie gras** and rub it through a clean fine wire sieve, and mix it with two wineglassfuls of sherry. Take half a pint of good-flavoured light stock, mix it with rather better than a quarter-ounce of Marshall's gelatine, and, when dissolved, strain and leave till somewhat cool;

whip it in a whipping-tin till quite spongy, add this to the **foie gras**, and pour it into the prepared mould; leave it on ice till cold and firm; then dip it into hot water, pass a clean cloth over the bottom to absorb any moisture, turn out the mousse on to a bed of plainly boiled cold rice, garnish it with little blocks of cut aspic jelly, and serve for a cold entree, or for second course, or any cold collation.

85. Mutton Chops, Maison d'Or

Neatly pare and flatten six tender mutton chops, make an incision crosswise in each, insert therein a slice of truffle, season with a teaspoon salt and half teaspoon pepper. Dip in beaten eggs, then roll in bread crumbs, place in a sautoir one beside another, with an ounce clarified butter, and fry for four minutes on each side. Arrange six heart-shaped bread croutons on a hot dish, arrange chops over, place a thin slice of paté de **foie gras** on top of each, pour a hot Madeira sauce around, adjust a paper frill at end bones of chops and serve.

86. Nerac Terrine

Take one or two fresh rabbits, skin and cleanse them and remove all the meat; weigh it, then pound or pass it twice through a mincing machine with double its weight of raw fat and lean ham or fresh pork; add a quarter-pound of any cleansed game or poultry livers to each pound of meat; rub all through a coarse wire sieve, then put the mixture into a basin and season it with pepper and salt, very finely chopped bayleaf and thyme. Line a terrine jar all round with the prepared farce about one inch thick, press it well to the jar with the hand (which should be constantly dipped into cold water) so as to make the mixture perfectly smooth; take some raw fillets of rabbit or chicken, or any kind of game or poultry, season them with pepper and salt and chopped herbs, and then proceed to fill up the jar thus: - Put a layer of the forcemeat and then a layer of the fillets, sprinkling them now and then with sherry, and in the centre put the contents of a small jar of paté de **foie gras**, and cover over the fillets with a layer of very finely cut slices of raw fat bacon; continue in this manner till the jar is full, then put on the top two or three bayleaves, a slice of bacon and a little sherry; cover with a stiff water paste about an inch thick, and tie a piece of buttered paper down over it. Stand the jar in a tin containing boiling water, place it in a moderate oven for about two and a half hours, when it should be removed and set aside till cold; remove the paste and bayleaf and bacon, pour a little warm lard over the top, and when this is set clean the jar and place it on a dish on a folded napkin or on a dish-paper. Serve for a ball supper, luncheon, or breakfast dish; it can also be used for serving in scallops, and can be masked with aspic if liked. The quantities given above are sufficient for ten to twelve persons, and if kept in a cool place will keep good for a week or so. If the lid is put on and fastened down air-tight the contents will keep a considerable time. The bones taken from the rabbits can be used for soups, sauces, etc.

87. NOISETTES OF LAMB, ROTHSCHILD STYLE

Bone a plump saddle of lamb, and cut from the loin slices 1 inch thick; trim nicely, sauté in butter, pour over truffle sauce and garnish with small patties (1 1/4 inches in diameter) filled with purée of paté de **foie gras**.

88. PAIN DE VOLAILLE AU FOIE GRAS

Prepare a good chicken cream mixture, and with this half fill a well buttered plain mould; turn out a small jar of paté de **foie gras** truffé, remove all the fat, etc, and place it in the centre of the mixture, covering it all up with more of the farce; poach or steam in the usual way, then turn out and serve with a rich Béchamel or Supreme sauce round it.

89. PATÉ DE FOIE GRAS

Have a **foie gras** weighing about a pound and a half. Make some forcemeat with one pound of turkey breast, one pound of fresh pork, mixed herbs, laurel leaves, thyme, salt, pepper, and two heads of cloves, and pound well. Peel one pound of truffles carefully, and stick some large pieces into the **foie gras**.

Line the bottom of a deep dish with some of the stuffing, lay the **foie gras** on this, surround it with the remainder of the truffles, fill up all interstices with the stuffing, and cover the whole with slices of bacon and laurel leaves. Cook the pie in. a bain-marie over a slow fire, keep the water at boiling point, but be careful none gets into the pie. It generally takes about an hour and a half to cook a pie of this size. Stick a skewer into the centre, and if burning hot when taken out you will know that the pie is done. When cold, remove the slices of bacon and cover with a layer of lard. Some people prefer the pie baked in the oven, as they consider it has more flavour. If the pie is to be eaten immediately, calfs liver forcemeat may be used, instead of turkey and pork, Gravy patties.

Line some small moulds with light paste, and fill with whatever forcemeat fancied, cover the moulds with paste, egg over, and bake; then remove the covers, scoop out the forcemeat, turn the patties out of the moulds, and fill them with well-seasoned, reduced gravy.

90. PÂTÉ DE FOIE GRAS CANAPÉS

For twenty-four sandwiches take one tureen of **foie gras**. Remove the fat, and mash the **foie gras** to a perfectly smooth paste, adding gradually four tablespoonfuls of soft, not melted, butter; add a dash of cayenne and a half teaspoonful of salt and about ten drops of onion juice, and press the whole through a sieve. Cut slices of bread into fancy shapes and toast; crescents are very pretty. Cover each slice thickly with this paste; garnish with hard-boiled white of egg, cut into diamonds or tiny crescents, and olives cut into rings. Arrange neatly, and they are ready to serve.

91. Paté De Foie Gras In Aspic Jelly

1 can paté de **foie gras**.
2 lbs. beef and bone from leg. 2 lbs. veal.
2 or 3 calves feet.
2 whites of eggs with shells.
1/2 chicken. 4 qts. water. 1 lemon. 1 pod pepper. 1 tablespoon salt.

Chop chicken and meat together with calves feet, water, salt and pepper, and let boil about 3 hours, strain and set aside until next day; then skim off the grease, put on to boil with lemon juice and eggs beaten to a froth and mashed shells, then strain again through a flannel dipped in ice water. When partially congealed pour into moulds, half filling them. Put slices of paté de **foie gras** on this and fill up with jelly, serve on lettuce leaves with mayonnaise. If you do not wish to use paté de **foie gras**, slice tomatoes or celery or shrimp cut fine, and mixed with mayonnaise is very nice.

92. Pheasant Pie à La Française

Take a square fleur mould, butter it inside, and place it on a baking-tin on a double fold of foolscap paper that is buttered; then line the mould about a quarter of an inch thick with short paste, pressing the paste well into the shape of the tin; take a picked, singed, cleansed and boned pheasant, cut it up in neat joints, lay these open and season them with a little mignonette pepper, a very little salt, and washed and chopped fresh mushroom, a little eschalot, thyme, bay leaf, parsley, and the livers of the pheasants finely chopped; place a little piece of paté de **foie gras** about the size of a Spanish nut in each piece of pheasant, and then roll up the pieces in cylinder shapes, and place these pieces one on the other in the pie until it is full. Wet the edge of the paste and roll out some more paste about half the thickness of that used for the lining of the mould, cover the pie over, and trim the edges; roll out the remainder of the paste perfectly thin like a wafer, and stamp it out in rounds about one and a half inches in diameter, and by means of a knife work out the rounds of paste in the form of small shells. Wet the top of the pie paste over with a little cold water, using a paste brush for the purpose, and then place the little shells on the top until it is quite covered; make a little hole in the centre of the top so as to be able to fill the pie up with gravy when cold; place a band of buttered paper round, so as to stand about three inches above the pie, and put it into a moderate oven, and bake for one and a half to two hours; during the baking keep the top of the pie covered over with a wetted paper to prevent the paste getting browned, as it should be a pretty fawn colour when cooked. Put it away till cold, then fill up with gravy made from the bones and then remove the tin from it; place the pie on a dish on a dish-paper, and garnish it round with nice blocks of cut Aspic Jelly, and serve for any cold collation, such as for supper, luncheon, race meetings, etc.

93. Pheasants à la Bohèmienne

Truss the pheasants, and stuff them with a forcemeat composed of chopped truffles, **foie gras**, salt, pepper, and mixed herbs, + Stew the pheasants in mirepoix, with a wine-glassful of Madeira; when done, serve garnished with stewed truffles, **foie gras**, cockscombs, and cock's kidneys; pass the sauce through a tammy, and pour over the birds.

94. Pigeons en Poqueton

Put some pâté de **foie gras** forcemeat, or any other forcemeat, into a small stewpan, and spread it all over at the bottom and sides, rubbing the stewpan first with butter. Put in a couple of pigeons trussed for roasting, some sweetbreads and tongue cut into neat pieces, and some button mushrooms; arrange all these tastily in the pan, place some more forcemeat on the top, cover it over with slices of bacon, and bake it in a gentle oven. Before closing it, pour some good gravy inside. The pigeons should be seasoned with pepper and salt, and just rubbed with garlic. When it is cooked, take it from the oven, and turn it carefully out into its dish, and pour a very rich sauce over it.

95. Plovers' Eggs In Aspic à La Victoria

Line both parts of the little egg moulds with aspic jelly, cut some small diamond shapes from hard-boiled white of egg and little rings from sliced truffle; arrange these in star shapes in the tops of the egg moulds, set these with a little aspic jelly, and garnish the moulds all over with little picked leaves of chervil (shreds of lettuce and tarragon may also be used); set this garnish with a little more aspic, place a plainly boiled plover's egg in the top of each mould, fix the two parts of the mould together, and carefully fill up with aspic jelly; put them aside on ice till set, then turn out. Prepare a piccolo border mould in the same manner by lining it with aspic jelly, and garnish it with stars and chervil, etc, similar to the little moulds, and fill it up with aspic; when it is set turn out and place one of the prepared eggs in each hollow of the piccolo border and one in the centre, and garnish the centre round the eggs and dish with chopped aspic, by means of a forcing bag and pipe, and blocks of **foie gras** at the corners of the piccolo shape as in engraving. Little green tarragon and chervil leaves may be placed here and there on the garnish.

96. Poached Eggs, à la Reine

Spread some purée de **foie gras** on a piece of toast. Put a poached egg on top, cover with cream sauce, and sprinkle with finely chopped truffles. After the truffles have been chopped put in a napkin and squeeze out the juice, and then chop again. They will then be dry, and easy to sprinkle.

97. Poached Eggs, Gourmet

Spread some paté de **foie gras** on four pieces of toast, lay a poached egg on top of each, and cover with Bearnaise sauce.

98. Poached Eggs, Perigordine

Spread some paté de **foie gras** on four pieces of toast, lay a poached egg on top of each, and cover with sauce Perigordine.

99. Poached Eggs, Talleyrand

On four round pieces of toast spread some **foie gras**, lay a poached egg on top of each piece, and cover with sauce Perigueux.

100. Potato Salad

Bake your potatoes, peel, and slice them. Cut up some truffles, which have been boiled in white wine, into very thin slices, and arrange them in alternate layers in a salad-bowl with the sliced potatoes; the last layer must be of truffles, garnish with cold boiled young onions, fillets of anchovy, and either stuffed or stoned olives, sprinkle with salt, pepper; season with olive oil and a little vinegar, and serve.

Turkey-hen stuffed with truffles; either roasted or braised.

Chop up some breasts of chicken, **foies gras**, bacon, and truffles, season with salt, pepper, and a laurel leaf, moisten with stock, add two or three dozen whole truffles, and simmer over a very slow fire for half an hour; when cold, place the forcemeat and truffles in a turkey-hen, trussed for roasting; sew up the pouch securely, and hang in a cool place for three or four days, after which, cover it with slices of bacon, and a buttered sheet of paper; when nearly done, remove the bacon and paper, and dish up the bird as soon as a good brown colour; add either some sliced or chopped truffles to the gravy, and hand in a sauceboat.

If you braise your turkey, cut up the breasts of chicken, bacon and **foie gras** into large dice.

101. PULLET À LA MONTMORENCY

Dress a large fat pullet, lard the breast and stuff it with **foie gras**, hard boiled eggs, and chopped bacon: cook and brown it like a fricandeau.

102. PURÉE FOR CUTLETS OF QUAILS À LA GREVILLE

Take, for six to eight persons, a small basket of fresh mushrooms, wash and cleanse them thoroughly, then press from the water and chop them up very fine; put them into a sauté pan with one and a half ounces of butter, one finely-chopped eschalot, and a little salt and pepper, and draw down on the side of the stove till the mushrooms are into a purée; then add two ounces of finely-chopped cooked ham, one ounce of freshly-made white bread-crumbs, two ounces of paté de **foie gras** that has been rubbed through a wire sieve, and a teaspoonful of warm glaze; mix together, and set aside in a cool place till firm, then use.

103. PUREE FOR LITTLE SWANS À LA PHRYGIENNE

Take, for eight to ten moulds, the contents of a small jar of paté de **foie gras** freed from fat, and six ounces of cooked chicken that has been pounded till quite smooth and rubbed through a fine hair sieve; mix these well together in the mortar, and add half a pint of strong good-flavoured warm chicken or other light stock that would set into a stiff jelly when cold, and use when setting.

104. QUAILS À LA LESSEPS

Take some boned quails with the feet left on, and place inside each bird a peeled dried raw potato, cut about two and a half inches long by one and a half wide, and formed into cylinder shapes; dry these with a cloth, and then rub them well over with butter; fasten up the birds in little bands of buttered paper, place them in a buttered sauté pan with half a wineglassful of sherry, and put in the oven for about fifteen minutes. When cooked, take up and put aside till cold, then remove the papers and the potatoes, and by means of a forcing bag and a plain pipe fill up the birds with a ragout, as below; put them in a cool place till the ragout is perfectly set, then cut the birds in half with a wet warm knife, and mask each over with brown Chaudfroid sauce ; when well coated lightly mask over with a little liquid Aspic jelly, and dish up round a timbal of clear ice prepared as below. Arrange between each half-bird a little finely-chopped aspic, and garnish the top of the birds with a little paté de **foie gras** that has been passed through a wire sieve, using a forcing bag and large rose pipe for the purpose; garnish the dish here and there with little sprigs of picked chervil and tarragon, and when about to serve put a lighted night-light in the centre of the ice timbal, and serve at once.

105. RAGOUT FOR EGGS IN CHAUDFROID

Take half a pint of good-flavoured chicken stock or clear soup that is quite in a jelly in strength equal to aspic, mix with it half a pint of stiffly-whipped double cream, a dust of coralline pepper and a little salt, one ounce of grated Parmesan cheese, three ounces of finely-minced cooked chicken, two ounces of lean cooked ham, minced, three hard-boiled yolks of eggs cut into tiny dice shapes, and two ounces of paté de **foie** grew that have been rubbed through a sieve; mix up well together, stir on ice till it begins to set, then use.

106. RAGOUT FOR FILLING THE QUAILS À LA LESSEPS

Take for four quails the half-breast of a cooked chicken (cut into small pieces), six button mushrooms, two or three truffles, and two ounces of **foie gras**; mix these with the sauce prepared as below[10], leave till nearly set, then use.

---

[10] « *Sauce for ragout for quails à la Lesseps:* Put a dessertspoonful of Bovril into a stewpan with a quarter-pint of Tomato sauce, a wineglassful of sherry, and half a pint of aspic jelly; reduce to half the quantity, keep skimmed while boiling, then tammy, and use.»

107. Ragout For Little Timbals à la Monaco

Take, for ten to twelve persons, the contents of a small jar of paté de **foie gras**, half a small cooked sweetbread, half a bottle of Financiere, one or two truffles and cooked button mushrooms (those left from a previous meal would do); cut these ingredients into small dice shapes, then prepare a Sauce, and when it is cooling mix in the above mixture, leave till nearly set, then fill up the moulds with it.

108. Ragout For Patties à la Montrose

Take some cold game or poultry, or roast mutton, beef, or lamb, and cut it into dice shapes, mix with it a very little good stock to moisten it, and a little cooked button mushrooms, truffle, ham, or **foie gras** may be added.

109. Reed birds in Aspic

Take the back and breast bone from a dozen birds, splitting them down the back first. Save the feet. Make a force-meat of *paté de **foie gras*** and panada in equal proportions; season highly, spread the inside of the birds, sew them up as nearly in shape as possible; bake seven to ten minutes, then dip them into glaze; put a little pale aspic in a dozen dariole moulds, enough to cover the bottom a quarter of an inch, and when just set put in a bird breast down; set on ice a few minutes, then pour in aspic to cover the bird a quarter of an inch. Put on ice. Turn out, and on the top of each strew pistachio nuts chopped very fine. Insert the two feet of the bird, scalded and dried, to stand up from the centre.

110. RILLETTES DE TOURS

(Cretons Canadiens) Three lbs. shoulder of fresh pork, 3 lbs. cutlets of pork, 1 filet of pork, 2 pork kidneys, 2 lbs. of kidney fat, 1 pint of water, 3 tablespoons of salt, pepper, and 4 onions minced fine with the pork fat. Chop the meat into small dice, mince the fat and kidneys very fine; let all boil gently for 4 hours. About 1/2 hour before removing from the fire, add 1 teaspoonful of mixed spices and 1/4 lb. fresh mushrooms cut in large pieces. Line a mould with half-set aspic; when set, pour in the mixture, pour over more aspic.

This is excellent for a cold supper or can be used as pâté de **foie gras**, and it may be moulded in buttered dishes without the aspic.

111. SALMI OF LARKS À LA MACÉDOINE, COLD

Take a dozen larks, bone and stuff them with pâté de **foie gras**, and make them as nearly as possible of the same size and shape. Make half a pint of brown sauce, adding a glass of sherry, a little mushroom ketchup, and an ounce of glaze; boil together, and reduce one half, adding a couple of spoonfuls of tomato juice; pass through a sieve, and, when nearly cold, add a gill of melted aspic. Mask the larks, and place them in a sauté pan, and cook them; take them out and remove neatly any surplus sauce, and dish them in the entrée dish in a circle. Take the contents of a tin of macédoine of vegetables boiled tender in a quart of water, add a dust of salt, a saltspoonful of sugar, and a piece of butter the size of a walnut; strain off, and, when cold, toss them in two tablespoonfuls of liquid aspic jelly. This macédoine should be piled up high and served in the centre. Garnish with chopped aspic round the larks, and sippets of aspic beyond this.

112. SALMIS OF SNIPE

Clean and roast lightly six snipe, saving the trail.

When done let them get cold, then cut them up and remove the skin, and lay them in a buttered stewpan; pound the trimmings and bones in a mortar, and put them into a stewpan with two shallots, a clove, a bouquet of herbs, and half a pint of claret; let this simmer until reduced to one half. Then add three quarters of a pint of Spanish sauce.

Let these *very gently simmer* for half an hour, skimming frequently; strain through a fine sieve, and return to the stewpan. If it is not thick enough to coat the spoon, reduce a little more. Pour this sauce over the snipe in the sauté pan, and let it get hot without boiling; pile the pieces in a pyramid; meanwhile chop the trail, mix with half the quantity of *pâté de **foie gras*** and a little salt and pepper; spread this on croûtons, bake, and use them to garnish the snipe.

113. Sandwiches à la Fiane

Take some little sandwich moulds, line them thinly with aspic jelly, ornament them with shreds of red French chilli, white of egg, and picked leaves of chervil, setting these with a little more aspic, partly fill the moulds with some thinly-cut slices of paté de **foie gras**. Line some more moulds with a plain aspic and fill these up with a purée of chicken or any white meat, let this partly set, then pour a little liquid aspic into the moulds containing the **foie gras**, and place those containing the chicken to those with the **foie gras**, then leave till set and firm, and when cold turn out the contents of each pair of moulds by dipping them in hot water, and place each on a fried crouton about the same size as the moulds. Dish up on a cold dish on a paper and garnish here and there with bunches of well-washed cress, and when in season quarters of boiled plover's egg that are sprinkled with a little of Marshall's Coralline Pepper. Serve as a cold entree for dinner, luncheon, or ball supper.

114. Savory Forcemeat

This forcemeat is composed of minced ham, onions, sweetbreads, truffles, and mushrooms. First warm the ham and onion in either melted butter or lard, add the other ingredients; moisten with stock, and boil; stir in some yolks of egg and lemon-juice before taking off the fire. Chicken's breasts, **foie gras**, kidneys, or cockscombs can be added to this forcemeat.

115. SCRAMBLED EGGS, SCHMIDT

Cut from a stale sandwich loaf six slices a quarter of an inch thick, toast to a nice golden colour, trim to two-inch-square pieces and spread a teaspoon paté de **foie** on top of each toast, arrange on a hot dish. Carefully crack eight fresh eggs in a bowl, add a half gill cream, half teaspoon salt and three saltspoons white pepper. Sharply beat up with a fork for one minute, heat a tablespoon butter in a frying pan, drop in the eggs and cook for six minutes, frequently stirring meanwhile. Evenly arrange them over the toasts and send to the table.

116. SKEWERS OF FAT GOOSE LIVER, VILLEROI STYLE

Proceed as above, using but **foie gras** and truffles. Note. - Skewers of sweetbread, of beef palate, of cocks' kidneys, etc., can be prepared as indicated above.

117. SMALL CAKES OF POTATOES

Place the meat on a **foie gras** toast, pour over Perigordine sauce and garnish with small crusts filled with purée of asparagus.

118. SMALL SNIPE PATTIES, EPICUREAN STYLE

Bone 8 or 10 snipe, and stuff them with chicken forcemeat, to which add one-eighth part of cooked forcemeat; lay a piece each of truffle and **foie gras** in each bird, and shape them in round balls.

Line some deep tartlet or patty moulds with short paste, place the snipe therein, and cover with a layer of paste, being careful to well close the borders. Make a small opening at the top and decorate the cover; then brush over with beaten egg, and bake in a moderate oven for 30 to 40 minutes.

With the bones of the birds prepare a rich stock, strain and reduce it with Madeira sauce.

When the birds are done lift the cover, pour over some of the gravy, and serve on a napkin.

Note. - This dish may be served cold by adding some gelatine to the stock before filling up the patties.

119. SMALL TENDERLOIN STEAK, RACHEL

Broil the steaks and lay on a platter. Put a slice of terrine de **foie gras** on top, garnish with peas au beurre and Julienne potatoes. Serve sauce Madere.

120. SOUFFLE OF FOIE GRAS À LA MONTREAL

Place a double band of paper round the outside of a silver or paper soufflé case, so that it stands about four inches above the case, fix it with a little sealing-wax, and then line it with a mock **foie gras** or liver farce, prepared as below[11], by means of a forcing bag with a plain pipe, forcing out the mixture to the thickness and length of finger biscuits; smooth this over with a wet warm knife, then fill up the inside of

---

[11] See the recipe *Cream mixture à la Montreal*.

the case with the cream mixture as below, and put the soufflé into the ice cave for about one hour; then remove the paper band, and garnish the top of the soufflé as in engraving with cooked artichoke bottoms that have been sliced and seasoned with a little salad oil, tarragon vinegar, chopped tarragon, and a little finely-chopped aspic jelly. Serve on a napkin or dish-paper for an entree or second-course dish, or for a cold collation.

121. SQUAB CUTLETS, SYLVIA STYLE

Split 6 squabs in halves and remove all bones except the drumsticks. Sauté the squabs lightly on the inner side only, and put them under light press. When cold, trim them nicely and lay on the inner side a salpicon of truffles, mushrooms and **foie gras** cut in small squares and mixed with well reduced German sauce. Cover with chicken forcemeat and decorate with truffles and smoked beef tongue to your fancy.

Lay the cutlets in a buttered sauté pan. Fifteen minutes before-serving put it on top of the range, and when the butter hisses cover the pan and finish to cook in a moderate oven. Dress on a dish, put on each drumstick a favor and serve truffle sauce separate.

122. STUFFED EGGS, EPICURE

Boil six eggs until hard, remove the shells, and cut in two lengthwise. Mix the yolks with one spoonful of purée de **foie gras**, and the chopped breast of a boiled chicken. Season with salt and pepper, pass through a fine sieve, put in bowl, add two ounces of sweet butter, mix well, and fill the eggs. Serve on lettuce leaves.

123. STUFFED PULLET

Bone the pullet, stuff with forcemeat made with minced veal, egg, ham, onions, **foie gras**, and mushrooms. First warm the veal, onion, and ham in melted butter, then add the mushrooms and **foie gras**, moisten with stock and boil. Stir in two yolks of eggs and a teaspoonful of lemon juice before taking off the fire, season with a little salt, pepper, and a pinch of nutmeg. After stuffing the fowl with this mixture, sew it up, turn the skin of the neck half over the head and cut off part of the comb, which will give it the appearance of a turtle's head. Blanch and singe four chickens' feet, cut off the claws and stick two where the wings ought to be and two in the thighs, so as to look like turtle's feet. Stew the pullet with a little ham, onions, and carrots, tossed previously in butter, moisten with stock, skim occasionally. When done, cut the string where it is sewn, lay it on its back in a dish, garnish the breast with sliced truffles cut in fancy shapes, and place a crayfish tail to represent the turtle's tail.

Velouté sauce may be handed with this dish, or it may be eaten cold and garnished with aspic.

124. Supreme De Volaille

For this the two sides of the breast of the fowl are lifted off in a piece and split in half (instead of being thinly sliced down), each being then cut in two, these fillets being placed in a well buttered baking dish with a very little lemon juice and chicken stock, covered with a buttered paper and cooked from eight to ten minutes, according to thickness; then dish them alternately with sliced hot cooked tongue cut to match, fill up the centre with a ragout of truffles, and pour sauce supreme round, sending more to table in a boat. French cooks look on a supreme de volaille as a masterpiece, and grudge neither trouble nor expense in preparing it. It is bound to be an expensive dish, as the breast only produces four, or at most eight fillets, though French chefs also use the filets mignons (or the portion answering to that name); moreover they shape the fillets most carefully into a pearshape, by batting and pressing them into shape with a hot wet knife. The sauce is the richest white sauce of the French cuisine, and according to some cooks should be made solely with chicken stock.

M. Gouffe however advises it being prepared thus: Put into a pan a gill of chicken glace, three gills of very carefully made velouté sauce (prepared with veal stock), and one quarter gill of essence of mushrooms; bring this all to a boil, then draw it to the side of the stove and let it simmer very gently for half an hour; after skimming it well, stir it gently over the fire till the sauce will mask the spoon, then dilute it a little with strong rich chicken stock. The supreme is always prepared thus, though its name may vary from the garnish served with it; as for instance supreme de volaille aux truffes (with a ragout of truffles in the centre); supreme à la royale (the fillets being served on a border of vegetables, with supreme sauce round, a macedoine of cooked vegetables being piled up in the centre); S. a l'ivoire (when the fillets cooked as above are mounted on a border of chicken farce, delicately flavoured with **foie gras**, a supreme sauce being poured over and round them, and the centre filled with either asparagus points, peas, or a macedoine of young spring vegetables); for the border prepare a farce of chicken as given in filets a l'ambassadrice, adding to it at the last two or three tablespoonfuls of cream, and fill a well buttered border mould with the mixture, putting in pretty freely small dice of paté de **foie gras** truffé (just taken from the pot, for if left standing they lose their aroma), cover with a buttered paper, and poach or steam till on touching the centre with your finger it feels firm.

This list might be prolonged to any extent, as, given the foundation described above, supreme can be varied indefinitely. It must be remembered that rabbits, partridges, pheasants, and indeed any kind of game, may be cooked like fowls, as fillets, whilst venison can follow the recipes given for mutton.

125. Surprise Eggs In Nest

Have ready 1 pound of chicken cream forcemeat; with 2 table spoons mould some egg-shaped quenelles, as described below:

Take one spoon filled with forcemeat in the left hand, make a hollow space in the center to lay therein a ball of purée of **foie gras**, cover with forcemeat and smooth the surface with a table knife dipped in luke warm water; with the other spoon, previously dipped in warm water, scoop out the quenelle and lay it in a buttered sauté pan. When a sufficient quantity of quenelles are made; set the pan on the fire, pour some boiling salted water on them, let come to a boil, and then remove the pan to the corner of the range to allow the quenelles to cook without boiling. After 10 minutes put them aside into a bowl; when cold, drain and dry them on a cloth; dip them in beaten eggs and roll in bread crumbs, and fry in hot lard to a nice golden hue.

Dress them in a nest made with Julienne potatoes, and serve separate some Pojarsky sauce.

126. Sweetbread, Junot Style

Cut some parboiled sweetbreads horizontally in halves, and sauté them in clarified butter (without browning) until they are cooked; put them under a light press, and when cold trim them to a nice oval shape.

Place on each half of sweetbread a salpicon of **foie gras** and truffles, and cover with chicken cream forcemeat. Smooth the surface and decorate nicely, then place in a buttered sauté pan and cook in a slow oven for 15 minutes. Serve with purée of mushrooms.

127. SWEETBREADS VICTOR EMMANUEL

Soak six large heart sweetbreads in cold water for two hours, drain, plunge in a quart boiling water with a teaspoon salt, boil for five minutes, drain on sieve, neatly trim all around and lard surface with a few strips of larding pork. Finely slice an ounce salt pork, a carrot, small onion, six fresh mushrooms, and place in a sautoire with a branch parsley and bay leaf. Lay breads on top, season with a teaspoon salt, lightly baste with butter and cook on fire for five minutes. Pour in one and a half gills white wine, let briskly reduce to almost a glaze, pour in one and a half gills broth, cover breasts with a sheet buttered paper, set in oven for twenty minutes, remove and keep hot.

Boil three ounces Italian rice in a pint broth with teaspoon salt for thirty-five minutes and drain on sieve. Place rice in a small saucepan with two truffles cut in small squares, two tablespoons paté de **foie gras**, four tablespoons sweetbreads gravy, an ounce grated Parmesan cheese and two egg yolks; season with two saltspoons salt, a saltspoon cayenne, and gently mix on fire while heating for five minutes. Arrange rice crown-like on a large hot dish and place sweetbreads in centre. Mix in small saucepan a tablespoon each good butter and flour. Skim fat off sweetbreads gravy, strain through cheesecloth into pan and add a gill cream and saltspoon cayenne. Mix well until it comes to a boil, let reduce for five minutes, add an egg yolk and sharply mix while heating for one minute. Pour sauce over sweetbreads in centre of rice, set in oven for ten minutes, remove and serve.

128. TERREEN OF PARTRIDGES, PARISIAN STYLE

Lift the breasts of 4 or 5 partridges; season and sauté them lightly, and set away to cool. Chop fine 8 ounces each of lean pork, fat pork and breast of fowl; add 2 ounces of cooked force-meat, and pound fine in the mortar; season with salt and allspice, and add 1/2 gill of sherry and a good dash of brandy.

Line a large terreen with thin slices of fat pork, and fill with alternate layers of forcemeat, breast of partridge, forcemeat, truffles and **foie gras**, forcemeat, and so on until the terreen is filled. Cover with slices of pork, cover the terreen, and hermetically seal it with paste.

Place the terreen in a pan partly filled with water and cook in a moderate oven for 2 hours and 30 minutes; allow to get cold, then take off the cover, remove the fat and fill with jelly made with the bones of the partridges.

129. TERRINE DE FOIE GRAS À LA GELÉE

Put the **foie gras** on ice for a few hours. Carve from the terrine with a table spoon and place on a platter covered with a napkin. Decorate with meat jelly cut in triangles and chopped, and parsley in branches.

130. TERRINE DE FOIE GRAS EN ASPIC

Use a jelly mould that will contain as much as six small individual moulds. Put a little melted, but not hot, meat jelly in the bottom, and set on cracked ice until it is firm. Cut some **foie gras** from a terrine with a spoon, and lay in the mould, then cover with a little more melted jelly, then another layer of **foie gras**, and so continue until the mould is full. Set in the ice box for an hour; and serve on a napkin, with parsley in branches.

131. TERRINE OF PLOVER

Cut heads and feet off six fat plovers, split open through backs without separating, draw and remove bones from breasts. Lay on a table, season with a half teaspoon salt, a saltspoon each cayenne, grated nutmeg and mixed spices, then spread a teaspoon of paté de **foie gras** over each. Cut a large truffle in six quarters, place one quarter over each bird, fold up and keep on a plate. Finely chop a pound each raw lean veal and fresh fat pork, place both in mortar with a teaspoon salt, two saltspoons cayenne, a saltspoon nutmeg and two egg yolks, pound to a very smooth pulp, add a half gill sherry, mix well, and rub force through sieve into a bowl. Line interior of an oval cocottc earthen tureen with thin slices larding pork, spread a layer of force at bottom and sides of tureen, place the six plovers in tureen crosswise, sprinkle over a tablespoon finely chopped truffle and fill tureen with balance of force, giving it a dome shape. Cover surface with thin slices of lard, place a sprig bay leaf on top, cover tureen, place in a roasting tin and pour hot water in pan up to two-thirds height of tureen. Set in oven for an hour and fifteen minutes, remove, place in a cool place and lift up cover.

Place a board same size as tureen over paté, lay a pound weight on it, keep in that condition until cold, turn paté on table, remove lard, and thoroughly wash and wipe inside of tureen. Set tureen on ice, pour in some melted jelly to quarter-inch thickness and let set. Cut a small truffle in. thin slices, then with small star cutter cut out as many star-like pieces as you can, place all around bottom of jelly, replace plovers in tureen, pour jelly all around edges and cover birds, etc., with it. When thoroughly set unmould on a cold dish with a folded napkin and serve.

132. TIMBALE OF PARTRIDGES

(French) Mince the raw flesh of two partridges, season, cut some truffles in small squares, ornament with them a buttered timbale-mould, half fill it with the farce, make a hollow in the centre of it allowing the farce to cover the sides of the mould to the top. Have ready a small ragoût of partridges, with slices of **foie gras** or truffles; the sauce should be thick, pour it into the empty centre of the mould, cover the whole with the remainder of the farce, then with a buttered paper. Poach the timbale in a covered bain-marie for thirty minutes in boiling water.

Turn it upon a dish and pour Madeira sauce round.

133. TIMBALS FOR CHICKEN À LA CHANCELIÈRE

Line some little timbal-moulds thinly with aspic jelly, garnish the tops with a little cut truffle, fill up with paté de **foie gras**, setting it with a little aspic jelly, and place the moulds aside till set; then dip into hot water, and turn out. Arrange these on the dish as shown in the engraving.

134. TIMBALS OF FOIE GRAS À LA BEATRICE

Line the little egg moulds very thinly with strong aspic jelly, then ornament them with finely-shredded raw crisp green lettuce, green French gherkins cut in shreds, and a little tarragon and red chilli; set these with a little aspic jelly, then fill up the centres with pieces of paté de **foie gras** and truffle cut in strips, add a little aspic jelly to set this, and put on ice to get cold. Line a piccolo border mould with aspic jelly, ornament it round the edge similarly to the eggs, then fill up with aspic and put aside to get cold; when ready to serve dip the moulds in warm water and turn out; arrange an egg shape in each of the spaces of the piccolo, put some chopped aspic in the centre by means of a forcing bag and pipe, and dish another egg on the top of this as in engraving; garnish round this with chopped aspic jelly, and quarters of plovers' or chicken's eggs, that are sprinkled with chopped truffle and shreds of red chilli and then masked with aspic jelly, and here and there some macedoine (or other nice vegetable), to a pint of which a tablespoonful of salad oil, a tablespoonful of tarragon vinegar, a few drops of chilli vinegar, and a pinch of mignonette pepper have been added. Place in each corner of the dish, as in engraving, a little round of thick Mayonnaise, using a forcing bag and pipe for the purpose, with some of the vegetables, and serve for a cold entree or for any cold collation.

135. TOURNEDOS, BAYARD

Season four small tenderloin steaks with salt and pepper. Heat two ounces of butter in a sauté pan, and sauté the fillets. Dress on toast spread with **foie gras**. Pour over them sauce Madere, to which has been added some sliced fresh mushrooms sauté in butter. Garnish with small round chicken croquettes, about one inch in diameter.

136. TOURNEDOS, CUSSY STYLE

Make a small horizontal incision on the side of the tournedos, passing the knife around, so as to divide the meat all over except on the border line; fill the tournedos with purée of **foie gras**; season with salt and pepper; dip in melted butter and bread crumbs, and broil over a brisk fire. Serve Perigueux sauce separate.

137. TOURNEDOS, ROSSINI

Cut from a two-pound piece well-trimmed tenderloin of beef six even slices, trim and neatly flatten them, season with a teaspoon salt and half teaspoon pepper, then lightly baste with oil. Arrange on broiler and broil over a brisk charcoal fire for three minutes on each side, remove and dress on a hot dish over six round pieces freshly prepared toasts. Dip a teaspoon in lukewarm water and scoop six thin pieces of paté de **foie gras** from a small tureen, arrange a piece on top of each filet, pour a hot Perigueux sauce over the filets, set in oven for two minutes and serve.

138. VOL AU VENT FINANCIÈRE

Prepare the pastry case, then have ready a ragout of tiny quenelles made of any raw. white meat, any remains of cooked brains or sweetbread, cut up small, little fillets of cooked chicken, small strips of cooked tongue, and, if at hand, a bottle of financiere garnish well drained, and heat all this in a rich velouté or béchamel, to which you add at the last the yolk of one or more eggs, beaten up with a spoonful or two of cream; then pour this all into the vol-au-vent, and serve at once. As a fact, anything can be used for a vol-au-vent, and it is a plat very dear to the thrifty French housewife in consequence, as it enables her to use up her scraps of all sorts in a dainty manner. The above is the regular vol-au-vent, to which oysters, prawns, truffles, mushrooms, **foie gras**, etc., may be added ad lib., but the culinary purist would call this, from its white sauce, a vol-au-vent Toulouse, a financiere ragout being strictly, served in a light brown sauce. Needless to say, small patties and cases may be filled in exactly the same way, and take their name from their filling; as for example, petite vol-au-vent aux huitres, when the cases are filled up with a rich and rather thick oyster sauce; aux crevettes, and de homard à la crème, when creamy shrimp or lobster sauce is used; or p. v. à la Montglas (minced chicken, tongue, truffle, etc., tossed in white or brown sauce); à la Milanaise (the filling consisting of shredded ham, chicken, truffles, macaroni, etc., tossed in white sauce strongly flavoured with grated Parmesan cheese); p. v. à la royale (filled with minced **foie gras**, chicken, sweetbreads, mushrooms, Ac., tossed in creamy béchamel sauce coloured with lobster butter); p. v. à la Valenciennes (filled with minced chicken, lobster, mushrooms, artichoke bottoms, and rice, all tossed in velouté rather strongly flavoured with curry butter); p. v. à la Barras (the filling consisting of turned olives cooked and heated in a bigarade sauce, with tiny fillets of cooked wild duck, or, indeed, duck of any kind); p. v. à la Lucullus (for this have some tiny quenelles poached in the usual way, and made from the crème mixture given in the chapter on soufflé's, etc., some cubes of **foie gras**, and three or four raw truffles cooked either in champagne or Rhine wine, and then sliced into julienne strips; put a spoonful of rather thick Champagne sauce into each patty, and on this place the quenelles and the **foie gras**, then the truffle julienne, and lastly a plover's egg, being careful to have everything very hot); finally, there are petits vol-au-vent à la menagère, when the cases are filled with a hot mince of any roast meat, heated in a good wine-flavoured sauce, a small poached egg being placed on the top just at the last instead of a cover, but this more properly belongs to the rechauffes.

Index of sources[12]

Beaty-Pownall, S., *Entrees*, Horace Cox, London 1901

Benton, J. Rosalie, *How To Cook Well*, D. Lothrop & Company, Boston 1886

Brisse, Léon, *366 menus and 1200 recipes of the Baron Brisse in French and English*, Sampson Low, Marston, Searle & Rivington, London 1884

Caron, Pierre, *French Dishes for American Tables*, D. Appleton, New York 1886

De Salis, Harriet Anne, *Dressed Game and Poultry à la Mode*, Longmans, London 1888

Farmer, Fannie Merritt, *The Boston Cooking-School Cook Book*, Little, Brown, and Company, Boston 1918

Filippini, Alexander, *300 Culinary Receipts*, H. M. Caldwell Company, New York 1892

Filippini, Alexander, *The Delmonico cook book. How to buy food, how to cook it, and how to serve it*, Brentano, London 1880

Filippini, Alexander, *The International Cook Book*, Doubleday, Page & Company, New York 1911

Harland, Marion - Terhune Herrick, Christine, *The National Cook Book*, Charles Scribner's Sons, New York 1896

---

[12] The following is a list of the printed sources used for the recipes.

Harland, Marion, *Common Sense In The Household. A Manual Of Practical Housewifery*, Charles Scribner's Sons, New York 1884

Harland, Marion, *Marion Harland's Complete Cook Book*, The Bobbs-Merrill Company, Indianapolis 1903

Harrison, Grace Clergue [Mrs., compiler], *Allied cookery, British, French, Italian, Belgian, Russian*, G.P. Putnam's sons, New York and London 1916

Hirtzler, Victor, *The Hotel St. Francis Cook Book*, The Hotel Monthly Press 1919

Kenney-Herbert, Arthur Robert, *Culinary Jottings*, Higginbotham And CO., Madras 1885

Marshall, A. B. [Mrs], *Larger Cookery Book Of Extra Recipes*, Marshall's School Of Cookery, London 1891

Meyer, Adolphe, *The Post-Graduate Cookery Book*, The Caterer Pub. Co, New york [1903?]

Owen, Catherine, *Choice Cookery*, Harper, New York 1889

Rorer, S. T., *Many Ways for Cooking Eggs*, Arnold and Co., Philadelphia 1907

Rorer, S. T., *Sandwiches*, Arnold and Co., Philadelphia [1911?]

Soyer, Alexis, *The Gastronomic Regenerator: A Simplified and Entirely New System of Cookery. With Nearly Two Thousand Practical Receipts Suited to the Income of All Classes*, Simpkin, Marshall & Co., London 1847

Stanford, Martha Pritchard, *The Old And New Cook Book*, Searcy, New Orleans 1904

Printed in Great Britain
by Amazon